DEMONSTRATING STUDENT SUCCESS

CONTENTS

11.   RESOURCES AND RECOMMENDATIONS FOR FUTURE
      PRACTICE   *167*

      APPENDIX A: SUGGESTED RESOURCES   *187*

      REFERENCES   *191*

      INDEX   *199*

ACKNOWLEDGMENTS

We wish to acknowledge the noteworthy efforts of the professionals listed in the dedication and applaud them for their success and their continuing efforts to address their challenges through the implementation of outcomes-based assessment. We appreciate their willingness to allow their peers and colleagues to get an honest glimpse of their trials and tribulations. Their honesty and willingness to share their own experiences, good and bad, will enhance and strengthen the work of others. It is only by learning from and working with others that we can continue to develop effective ways to empirically demonstrate that the cocurriculum plays a significant role in student learning and development.

Additionally, we thank Nasser A. Razek and Liuttui Cao for their support and assistance with this book. Their continuous efforts enabled us to realize our goals in an organized and timely manner. And as always, we are grateful for the support of our colleagues, students, family, and friends without whose understanding would make our goal of writing this book ever more challenging.

PREFACE

Over a decade and a half after Astin (1990) shared his thoughts about assessing student learning in *Assessment for Excellence* and almost as many years after Upcraft and Schuh (1996) and Palomba and Banta (1999) contributed their insights to the conversation, student affairs professionals continue to rely on these texts to guide their work in assessment. These, and many other works, provide a solid foundation of information regarding assessment in student affairs. However, increasing emphasis on the demonstration of student learning by institutions of higher education and the growing demand for accountability by stakeholders warranted the development of this practical guide. A how-to book for outcomes-based assessment in student affairs, this book is designed to give pragmatic advice when implementing assessment of student learning and development.

A Reference, Resource, and Tool for Reflection

It is our intention for this book to serve as a resource for current and future student affairs practitioners and faculty engaging in outcomes-based assessment. Each section provides insight into an important piece of the assessment puzzle beginning with the history of assessment, moving to how to effectively partake in outcomes-based assessment, and concluding with strategies for addressing challenges and suggestions for the future. We additionally provide excerpts from case studies to reinforce concepts introduced in this book to illustrate current practices in student affairs assessment and to offer realistic examples. We share these cases to assist administrators and faculty with the assessment and evaluation of student learning and development in the cocurricular environment. The case studies highlight what was learned during the outcomes-based assessment process and provide insights to help you with any challenges. The case studies are presented in further detail in Bresciani, Moore Gardner, and Hickmott's (2009) *Case Studies in Implementing Assessment in Student Affairs*. It is our intention for these books to be used in tandem to enhance and inspire the reader's work with outcomes-based assessment.

Additionally, we hope the reader will discover several ways to evaluate student learning and development in student affairs. Each case varies with regard to institutional type and approach, and each contributing author shares some tips for implementing outcomes-based assessment through a distinctive institutional lens. Purposeful in design, the diverse array of examples provide almost all readers with insights that can be incorporated into their work in their own unique campus environments.

Review of Chapters

This book is broken up into three parts. In the first part, "The Evolution and Significance of Outcomes-Based Assessment," chapter 1 offers a brief review of the history of outcomes-based assessment. Chapter 2 presents a definition and theoretical framework of outcomes-based assessment and discusses the difference between assessment and evaluation. The relationship between outcomes-based assessment and institutional accountability is explored, and the impact the process can have on planning, policy making, programming, and budgeting is described.

Part 2, "Effective Outcomes-Based Assessment," includes chapters 3 through 7. Chapter 3 details the components of an effective assessment plan, including defining goals and developing learning outcomes. Chapter 4 examines the myriad of assessment methods available and focuses on the need to consider the scope of the assessment prior to selecting a particular methodology. In chapter 5, we discuss how to use and disseminate results effectively. Issues to consider when communicating the findings of the assessment process are also included. We move on to the ins and outs of implementing outcomes-based assessment in student affairs in chapter 6. Chapter 6 also identifies the common challenges that arise during the implementation phase, considers the key stakeholders in the implementation process, and introduces strategies to help student affairs professionals employ assessment of student learning. Finally, chapter 7 concludes this section by reviewing the criteria for evaluating outcomes-based assessment within student affairs, as well as guidelines for promoting reflection and subsequent institutional assessment.

Part 3, "Barriers, Resources, and Future Considerations," includes chapters 8 through 11. Chapter 8 examines the variety of barriers to effective assessment and provides strategies for addressing potential challenges. Chapter 9 describes issues around collaboration, common barriers to collaboration, steps to establishing sustainable collaborations, and examples of successful collaboration. Chapter 10 deals with funding and provides recommendations on how to make the best use of human resources and time to achieve the most thorough and well-thought-out assessment process possible and do so cost effectively. The book concludes with chapter 11, which considers implications for future work, as well as introduces additional resources not covered in any of the preceding chapters.

Criteria for and Selection of Participating Institutions

The criteria that frame the institutional good practices discussed in this book are informed by the following four primary assessment sources:

1. *Nine Principles of Good Practice for Assessing Student Learning* by the American Association of Higher Education (1992)
2. *Outcomes-Based Academic and Co-curricular Program Review: A Compilation of Institutional Good Practices* by Bresciani (2006)
3. *Assessing Conditions to Enhance Educational Effectiveness: The Inventory for Student Engagement and Success* by Kuh, Kinzie, Schuh, Whitt, and Associates (2005)
4. *Assessment Essentials: Planning, Implementing, and Improving Assessment in Higher Education* by Palomba and Banta (1999)

The seven key criteria employed to determine the inclusion of the cases discussed in this book are

1. Demonstration that institutional stakeholders had a clear understanding of expectations for student learning and how the program review process would be used to improve learning;
2. Evidence of collaboration with various members of the university or college community to improve student learning;
3. The creation and implementation of methods that fit the nature of the assessment process and provided useful information;

4. Movement beyond simply getting results to actually using results to improve practice and enhance student learning and development;

5. Receipt of recognition or resources an institution or department received for assessment work or improvement in program or student learning;

6. Efficient use of human and financial resources used to support the assessment or program review process or improve student learning;

7. Demonstration of such qualities in coordinating the process, such as flexibility of approach while being systematic, adaptation to context, effectiveness, and efficiency.

These criteria are examined in detail in chapter 7.

Participating Institutions

An open invitation for submission of a case study was extended to all institutions that belong to the National Association of Student Personnel Administrators (NASPA) via an avenue approved by the NASPA office. Additionally, institutions recognized for their work in outcomes-based assessment, identified either through the recommendations of other assessment professionals or from the evidence of institutional Web sites, were invited to submit materials for this study. Each potential participating institution submitted a case study detailing its assessment and program review efforts. A detailed review of each of these cases is provided in Bresciani et al. After careful analysis using the aforementioned criteria, case studies were selected for inclusion in this book. The institutions and professionals who submitted the case studies are

Alverno College—Virginia Wagner
California State University, Sacramento—Lori E. Varlotta
Colorado State University—David A. McKelfresh and Kim K. Bender
Frederick Community College—L. Richard Haney and Debralee McClellan
Isothermal Community College—Karen Jones
John Carroll University—Kathleen Lis Dean, Patrick Rombalski, Kyle O'Dell, Lisa Ramsey, and John Scarano
North Carolina State University—Carrie Zelna

Northern Arizona University—Michael F. Butcher, Margot Saltonstall, Sarah Bickel, and Rick Brandel

Oregon State University—Rebecca A. Sanderson and Patricia Ketcham

Paradise Valley Community College—Paul A. Dale

Pennsylvania State University—Philip J. Burlingame and Andrea L. Dowhower

Texas A&M University—Sandi Osters

Widener University—Brigitte Valesey and Jo Allen

PART ONE

THE EVOLUTION AND SIGNIFICANCE OF OUTCOMES-BASED ASSESSMENT

I

HISTORY AND DEVELOPMENT OF OUTCOMES-BASED ASSESSMENT

While the upsurge of attention to assessment during the past few decades might lead many to believe it is a relatively new phenomenon in higher education, history reveals that assessment and higher education were intertwined well before the establishment of American higher education and the founding of the colonial colleges beginning in 1636.

As early as 1063 CE, the University of Bologna used "juried reviews" to demonstrate student learning. Oral recitation was often relied upon to highlight learning as far back as the days of Plato and Aristotle (Bresciani, 2006; Cohen, 1998; Lucas, 1994; Rudolph, 1990; Thelin, 2004). During colonial times in the United States, for example, faculty members at Harvard University required all students to demonstrate the acquisition of knowledge by participating in weekly disputes (Cohen).

It is important to note, however, that these early assessments were generally centered in a traditional classroom setting and not in the cocurricular environment. Written tests and oral recitations are two of the most common means of assessing learning inside the classroom that can be traced for hundreds of years. The cocurricular environment does not have such a rich history because often the significant amount of learning and development that takes place in residence halls, on soccer teams, or in student government has been left by the wayside. What follows is an overview of the history and foundations of outcomes-based assessment and an examination of the reasons behind the move toward purposefully assessing learning inside and outside the classroom.

Foundations

The outcomes-based assessment movement in the United States has its foundations in the educational and development psychology work of the 1930s and 1940s (Ewell, 2002; Kuh, Gonyea, & Rodriguez, 2002). Research at that time focused on student motivation and performance, along with a desire to enhance and advance how students learned. However, this research focused primarily on the traditional college student (18- to 22-year-olds) and only on those living in residential college environments. Feldman and Newcomb (1969, 1994) synthesized a notable amount of this research.

A number of other texts played a role in the history of assessment. In the 1970s, Astin (1977) published *What Matters Most in College: Four Critical Years*, a work he updated in 1993, which introduced the concept of the *value-added* approach to assessment and used longitudinal research about the impact of the college environment on students. This concept was introduced as a different way of demonstrating excellence in higher education. Individual student talents are the focus of this concept, and the quality of a college or university may be determined by the level of the positive impact the institution has on the development of those talents and the overall learning and development of students in general. More specifically, Astin (1991) described value-added assessment (also known as talent development, pretest-posttest, and longitudinal assessment) as assessing the same student or students repeatedly and over a period of time to determine how a particular experience (e.g., college attendance) has affected the student's growth and development. This particular design for assessment is considered advantageous because of its focus on change and development over time as well as its attention to the input characteristics students bring with them to college (e.g., academic preparation, socioeconomic status, parent's educational background, race, and gender), which play a key role in growth and development during college (Astin). Often referred to as the Inputs-Environment-Outputs Model (I-E-O), this form of assessing student learning often employs vigorous research methodology and provides the foundation for outcomes-based assessment programs today.

Following Astin (1977), Bowen (1977) took a different approach to assessment in higher education by introducing the relationship between public policy and assessment, and examining postsecondary learning from the perspective of higher education as a public good (Ewell, 2002). Ewell further explained that Bowen's book "helped establish a public policy context for assessment by emphasizing the societal returns on investment associated with higher education" (p. 4). These researchers were followed by a third approach in the 1970s, as Pace (1979) described the impact of college environments on student behavior in *Measuring Outcomes of College*. According to Ewell, the student learning research tradition contributed to outcomes-based assessment conceptually and methodologically with "basic taxonomies of outcomes, models of student growth and development, and tools for research like cognitive examinations, longitudinal and cross-sectional surveys, and quasi-experimental designs" (p. 4).

Retention and Student Behavior Research

Student learning research about retention and student behavior began in the 1960s and 1970s and had an impact on assessment in noteworthy ways. Ewell (2002) highlights three features of retention and student behavior research commonly mirrored in assessment work. The first was Tinto's (1975) idea that students who are academically and socially integrated into campus will have a higher rate of retention than those who are not. This belief was "useful in guiding applied research on student learning" (Ewell, p. 4). The next feature was the opportunity to test new methodologies for longitudinal student attrition research (e.g., specially configured surveys and multivariate analytical techniques). Such methodologies enabled researchers to gather information-rich data about student retention, which contributed to the development of strategies and support systems for students who have historically struggled to be retained. These methods, once tested and found valid and reliable, served as useful tools for assessing student learning. Finally, "retention scholarship was action research: though theoretically grounded and methodologically sophisticated, its object was always informed intervention" (Ewell, pp. 4–5). These features, when combined, act as a model of applied scholarship that is the foundation for many assessment practitioners today. Outcomes-based assessment of student learning is often geared toward determining what students learn in a particular situation or how they develop over time as a result of participation in a specific activity or experience. Moreover, it is completed most often with the intention of intervening while the student is still enrolled in the institution in an effort to enhance overall learning and development.

Scientific Management Theory

In addition to the development of the student learning, retention, and behavior literature of the 1960s and 1970s, *scientific management theory* was introduced to higher education through practices such as program review, strategic planning, and budgeting (Ewell, 2002). The basic ideas of this theory were developed by Frederick Taylor (1911), who asserted that decisions or processes should be based on formal theories or developed after effectively studying individuals in the workplace, as opposed to using informal theories or rules of thumb. By doing this, Taylor believed that the workplace could be organized in such a way as to produce maximum output with minimum effort. These ideas were transferred to the higher education setting by professionals who were interested in actually quantifying student learning and development in an effort to test and support the assumptions of learning that had existed since the onset of higher education.

According to Ewell (2002), scientific management used a "systems thinking" approach. In this approach, a system is thought to be made up of subsystems that provide inputs and generate outputs. The subsystems are interconnected and interdependent and create a holistic system. Systems thinking, asserts Ewell, focuses attention on student outcomes, thereby providing an end product for those interested (e.g., government, public stakeholders) in the social return on the investment of or in higher education. For example, within the system of a university or college, many subsystems (e.g., student activities, residence life, campus ministry, athletics) work together and individually to foster student learning and development and result in individual and systemwide learning. It is important to consider the impact of the subsystem as well as the system in general when determining the outcomes of student learning. We discuss this concept more later in this book. As we do so, we refer to the systems and subsystems as the *scope* of the assessment process or project.

The incorporation of scientific management theory in higher education also resulted in the development of numerous survey instruments focused on how students used campus programs and services and what their satisfaction level was regarding those programs. Moreover, according to Ewell (2002), the adoption of scientific management theory in higher education resulted in the creation of classification systems, or taxonomies, for student learning outcomes. Such taxonomies might include categories such as academic learning (communication skills, content knowledge), career skills (knowledge specific to a career or occupation, motivation to perform at a certain level, reliability), and personal development (cognitive or affective skills and attributes).

Program evaluation subsequently contributed to the evolution of assessment of student learning by providing higher education professionals with a set of models and vocabularies later used in assessment. The models and vocabularies started out quantitative in nature (Light, Singer, & Willett, 1990) but were later expanded to include qualitative methods (Creswell, 1998; Denzin & Lincoln, 2000; Guba & Lincoln, 1981; Patton, 2002). This was significant in that it provided professionals with a common language and set of methods to use when engaging in assessment of student learning.

Total Quality Management and Continuous Quality Improvement

The beginning of the 1990s ushered in a new set of ideas taken from the world of business. The intent of these business processes was to address organizational and administrative operations; they were known as Total Quality Management (TQM). TQM, later relabeled Continuous Quality Improvement (CQI) by the American Association of Higher Education, was universal in approach and viewed organizational change as imperative for success and survival (Ewell, 2002). In addition to both of them being systemic in nature, TQM/CQI and assessment had many similar attributes. According to Ewell, each "emphasized the need to listen carefully to those whom the system was trying to serve" and "both held that concrete information about performance was a critical part of a continuous cycle of planning and improvement" (p. 19).

Despite the commonalities of the two ideas, attempts to combine assessment and TQM/CQI did not see much success on college and university campuses. TQM/CQI did, however, reinforce the utility of and need for data collection about outcomes and processes on college and university campuses. Additionally, TQM/CQI introduced the idea of the student as a "customer" with a voice about the quality of programs and services produced by colleges and universities (Ewell, 2002). Finally, this concept helped to shift the focus from teaching to student learning and opened the door to a greater paradigm shift that is discussed in the following section.

Teaching to Learning Paradigm

In 1995 Barr and Tagg proposed a subtle yet significant paradigm shift in American higher education. According to Barr and Tagg, the paradigm that had historically governed higher education suggested that the business or function of colleges and universities was *to provide instruction.* This is referred to by Barr and Tagg as the *Instruction Paradigm.* Under this paradigm, teaching was believed to fit into the traditional 50-minute lecture delivered by the professor who stood at the front of the classroom sharing his or her knowledge before rows of seated students.

The new Learning Paradigm proposed by Barr and Tagg (1995) viewed colleges and universities as dynamic entities with the goal of *producing learning* rather than instruction. This paradigm encouraged creating the opportunity for learning, taking into account students' learning styles and preferences. According to this paradigm, the institution itself is in a constant state of learning, and over time the institution understands how to facilitate more learning with each new student or graduating class.

This concept was introduced earlier by Papert (1991) through the epistemology of situational constructivist learning in which the instructor purposefully creates the environment for learning. The student is presented with the intentionally designed learning opportunity and constructs the learning. The purposefully created learning environment changes subtly each time a new set of students is introduced to the environment. Furthermore, according to Barr and Tagg (1995), as the instructor learns more about how those students learn, he or she adjusts the learning environment to enhance the students' ability to construct learning.

Barr and Tagg (1995) argued that the shift from teaching to learning was not only important but inevitable because of a widening gap between what higher education claims to do and what it actually does. This paradigm shift contributed significantly to assessment as we know it today by changing the focus from the inputs of higher education (e.g., students and faculty) to the overall experience of higher education (e.g., instruction and the cocurricular experience) in order to evaluate the outputs of higher education (e.g., the learning and development that is produced). With this shift to evaluating the outcomes of higher education (student learning and development gained) came an increased understanding and awareness of the idea that learning can take many different forms and can even take place outside traditional classroom walls in the cocurricular environment (Astin, 1993; Kuh, Schuh, Whitt, & Associates, 1991). Additionally, this shift increased the institutional and individual accountability for student learning and helped move it to the forefront of the higher education enterprise (Ewell, 1997).

Assessment as a Movement

During the last decades of the 20th century, assessment became prominent in American higher education as financial resources became even scarcer and the pressure grew for Americans to compete in the global market. According to Ewell (2005), assessment emerged as a significant topic of policy discussion, demonstrated by legislators and other members of state and federal governments demanding greater accountability within higher education institutions. These policy makers also called for direct, tangible evidence of learning in the postsecondary arena.

Ewell (2002) describes the historical evolution of the interconnectedness of accountability and assessment using two *rounds*. Round 1 begins in the mid-1980s when two divergent ideologies of assessment became hot topics in higher education. The first, according to Ewell (2002), was a response to the curricular reform movements that took place at the end of the 1970s and beginning of the 1980s called *Involvement in Learning*. This report, published in 1984 by the Study Group on the Conditions of Excellence in American Higher Education, "argued that breakthrough improvements in undergraduate education could be achieved by establishing high expectations, deploying active and engaging pedagogies, and providing frequent feedback about performance" (Ewell, 2005, p. 107). The report then suggested that institutions of higher education use the feedback about student learning and development to inform and improve their own work (Ewell, 2002).

This report acted as the stimulus for the First National Conference on Assessment in Higher Education, which was cosponsored by the National Institute of Education and the American Association for Higher Education in 1985 (Ewell, 2002). This conference is considered by many to be the beginning of the higher education assessment movement, a movement well known for its often conflicting political and intellectual traditions. The divergence in viewpoints is illustrated by the two ideologies represented by *Involvement in Learning* and then *Time for Results* (National Governors' Association, 1986).

The second ideology was a result of the significant state interest in educational reform in the wake of *A Nation at Risk* (1983), which was a report on the K–12 sector of education, and by the National Governors' Association (1986) report *Time for Results*. This report called for institutions of higher education to become accountable to the public and to demonstrate this by setting clear standards for student learning and by making the results of the assessments of student learning available to the public (Ewell, 2005). *Time for Results* argued that institutions of higher education were "learning organizations" that should be motivated and directed by concrete information about student performance derived through assessment. The report advocated colleges and universities using the techniques of educational research and the social sciences to collect valid and reliable information about student performance that could then be used to inform institutional improvement. Additionally, it was proposed in the report that colleges and universities could effectively create systems to collect and process information about student learning and create decision-making systems capable of acting on it. A key point of this document was that information about student learning outcomes, when open and accessible to the public, would encourage improved performance and serve a public good (Ewell, 2005).

Contrary to the response many had hoped for, only a few institutions heeded the challenge. According to Hutchings and Marchese (1990), a number of colleges and universities opted not to respond and instead waited to see how the policy and push for accountability would play out. State leaders in turn were faced with the issue of varying institutional cooperation and the question of how to address the apathy displayed by American higher education in regard to assessment (Ewell, 2005; Hutchings & Marchese; Upcraft & Schuh, 1996).

Of great concern during this time was the separation of the contexts in which assessment was discussed. Referring to Ewell's (2005) Round 1 scenario, we see assessment identified as a systematic process for continuous improvement where programs were responsible for what they evaluated and the decisions that resulted. In Ewell's Round 2 scenario, we see the push for public accountability, with the stated aim of enabling comparison of assessment results of institutions. The desire to compare institutional results conflicted with the practice of conducting assessment to improve programs.

In an effort to avoid the forms of outcomes testing used in primary and secondary education, many public institutions agreed to participate in local assessment programs and to make the results of those assessments readily available to the public for review. Initially, this process met the demands for public accountability and kept the control of assessment within the institution. By 1990 a large portion of all colleges and universities participated in some form of institutional assessment, two-thirds of which stemmed from state mandates (Ewell, 2005). The local assessment approach that was embraced by many, however, was not found acceptable by all members of university and college communities.

According to Ewell (2005), many faculty members argued that assessment infringed on their right to determine what and how to teach, and others believed assessment was a trend that would dissipate with time. In addition to institutional dissonance, many state governments struggled with how to synthesize the assessment results coming from such different measures of outcomes in a way that was meaningful and useful to the public at large (Ewell, 1991). A final blow to the assessment mandates of the 1980s was the recession that was readily apparent by the end of that decade. With the recession came a shift in focus from "investing in higher education as a public good" to one of "gaining efficiencies in a large and expensive public enterprise" (Ewell, 2005, p. 112).

Round 2 of the relationship between assessment and accountability as described by Ewell (2005) actually began in 1985 but was not taken seriously until the mid-1990s when regional accreditation took over as the main external impetus behind institutional assessment. Even at this point, however, this relationship continued to go unnoticed or was altogether ignored for many more years. The relationship between peer review and accountability had its roots in the 1980s when peer review began as a means of evaluating the quality and effectiveness of academic programs and services (Ewell, 2002, 2005). In response to the accrediting requirements of the 1990s, institutions began establishing learning outcomes and employed various tools for gathering evidence of those outcomes and for disseminating and using the results.

Despite the intent of focusing on student learning, the accrediting organizations focused more on the process of peer review of the institution's overall self-reflection process than on the student learning outcomes. As a result, the actual results of learning were not at the forefront of the assessment process. Rather, accrediting agencies emphasized how institutions used the results of their assessments, not what students actually had learned (Ewell, 2005). This focus on process, however, did lead to an increased attention to outcomes-based decision making and planning in colleges and universities. Despite the shift from state-mandated assessment to peer review, many faculty continued to question the merit of assessment, viewing it more as an administrative process than an academic priority (Ewell, 2005).

A New Era of Assessment

The dawning of the new millennium brought with it even more changes for outcomes-based assessment in American higher education. Considerable changes in accreditation took place in an effort to provide institutions with meaningful and useful information. Compliance was separated from the "self-study" functions of accreditation, and the teaching and learning process became a central focus of accrediting teams (Ewell, 2005). Accreditors emphasized new language that underlined "*standards* for learning embedded directly into the curriculum and used to align day-to-day teaching and learning activities" (Ewell, p. 116). This new language shifted the focus of accreditation from organizational management, which viewed the existence of assessment as evidence of accountability, toward academic standards and curricular alignment as proof of accountability (Ewell).

In addition to the change in the focus of accreditation, assessment of the out-of-class experience became an even greater priority as resources dwindled and concerns about accountability continued to grow (Burke, 2005; Palomba & Banta, 1999; Upcraft & Schuh, 1996). Student affairs practitioners began the arduous process of defining learning outside the classroom and of creating methods and tools that would provide tangible and useful results. Despite a desire by many to actively engage in quality assessment of student learning outside the classroom, progress remains slow and assessment remains a daunting task to many.

We currently face a mix of accountability demands, accreditation standards, and outcomes-based assessment of student learning. State and federal governments continue to question whether institutions of higher education actually produce the learning that has for centuries been assumed. Accrediting bodies, likewise, want proof that colleges and universities are doing what is necessary to ensure that the full cognitive, affective, and social development of students is realized. Therefore, it is important that student affairs professionals accurately and effectively identify the quality of their contributions to student learning and development.

Outcomes-based assessment provides a means for addressing a number of the concerns highlighted in the preceding paragraphs. While the time, effort, and resources required to engage in effective outcomes-based assessment may seem daunting to already overtaxed higher education professionals, it is nevertheless important that student affairs professionals become well versed in the assessment of student learning to ensure that the true value of the cocurricular experience is not lost or misunderstood by external stakeholders, particularly in a time where available resources are growing even scarcer.

The chapters that follow provide the needed resources, ideas, and tools for those looking to engage in effective outcomes-based assessment. Examples from institutions engaging in outcomes-based assessment are provided to demonstrate the myriad of ways institutions can and do implement effective assessment programs. It is our hope that the information provided will equip the reader with the skills and knowledge needed to effectively identify student learning within student affairs at his or her campus.

2

DEFINITION AND RATIONALE
FOR OUTCOMES-BASED
ASSESSMENT

Before delving further into the world of outcomes-based assessment, it is important to establish common terminology that will be used throughout this book. There are a number of definitions for the terms *assessment* and *outcomes-based assessment*. These definitions vary in scope and foundation. As a result, the definition adopted by one institution may differ from that at another institution (Palomba & Banta, 1999; Schuh, Upcraft, & Associates, 2001). Regardless of any specific definition, outcomes-based assessment is about improving student success and informing improvements in the practice of student services and programming.

Upcraft and Schuh (1996) define assessment as "any effort to gather, analyze, and interpret evidence which describes institutional, divisional, or agency effectiveness" (p. 18). Maki (2004) presents a different perspective and describes assessment as a systematic process that examines the degree to which students learn when compared to the learning objectives described by educators. Palomba and Banta (1999) define assessment as "the systematic collection, review and use of information about educational programs undertaken for the purpose of improving student learning and development" (p. 4). These are just a few of the many definitions for assessment of student learning. For the sake of consistency, this book adopts Bresciani's (2006) definition of outcomes-based assessment as its starting point. According to Bresciani, outcomes-based assessment is a systematic and intentional process. In this process, student affairs professionals

articulate what the program intends to accomplish in regard to its services, research, student learning, and faculty/staff development programs. The faculty and/or professionals then purposefully plan the program so that the intended results (e.g., outcomes) can be achieved; implement methods to systematically—over time—identify whether end results *have* been achieved; and, finally, use the results to plan improvements or make recommendations for policy consideration, recruitment, retention, resource reallocation, or new resource requests. This systematic process of evaluation is then repeated at a later date to determine whether the program improvements contribute to intended outcomes. (p. 14)

Outcomes-based assessment uses the results of assessment to change and improve how a program, a department, a division, or an institution contributes to student learning. This process goes one step beyond typical evaluation (explained on pp. 18–20) by examining the program improvements after they are implemented to determine whether the improvements enhanced or contributed to students' learning and development.

Outcomes-based assessment is designed as a systematic and critical process that yields information about what programs, services, or functions of a student affairs department or division positively contribute to students' learning and success, and which ones should be improved (Bresciani, 2006; Maki, 2004; Suskie, 2004). Maki outlines two types of assessment that may be used when seeking information about the types and levels of learning produced or enhanced by a student affairs program, service, or function. Formative assessment is "designed to capture students' progress toward institution- or program-level outcomes" (p. 4) and provides proof of learning as a student progresses through a particular learning experience. For example, student leaders might receive regular feedback from their adviser about their ability to effectively manage a group meeting. This feedback is based on adviser and/or peer observations that are informed by a criteria checklist or rubric. After each meeting, the leaders may meet with their advisers to ascertain the feedback and then incorporate any changes in their leadership style prior to the next meeting. This enables the student leaders to continuously learn throughout the duration of their leadership experiences and apply any changes necessary, as opposed to only receiving feedback at the end.

Summative assessment, on the other hand, is "designed to capture students' achievement at the end of their program of study" (Maki, 2004, p. 6) and provides evidence of how well students master particular skills or knowledge (Maki). The results of summative assessment may be used to inform curricular, cocurricular, pedagogical, programmatic, and service changes if the data are collected in a manner where the location of those improvements can be identified. For example, faculty might administer comprehensive exams to demonstrate overall student learning while student affairs professionals might have senior resident assistants develop the training program for new resident assistants to demonstrate their mastery of the policies, information, and skills necessary to be an effective resident assistant. It is important that student affairs professionals consider and use both types of outcomes-based assessment to gain a complete picture of student learning on a particular campus.

When beginning any assessment process, the problem, need, or issue that serves as the foundation of the assessment should be determined (Banta, 2002; Banta & Associates, 2004; Bresciani, 2006; Maki, 2004; Palomba & Banta, 1999; Schuh, Upcraft, & Associates, 2001; Upcraft & Schuh, 1996). The purpose for the assessment is then derived from this problem, issue, or need and serves as the foundation of the assessment process. Determining who will be evaluated and how the assessment process will be designed are the next steps in the process. During this stage, stakeholders, including student affairs practitioners, faculty members, students, and administrators, should be considered and involved to ensure that everyone's needs are met and to ensure that support for the assessment is established. These stakeholders should all be included early in the assessment process. Students, for example, may provide a great deal of information about the issues, problems, or needs that should be addressed by the outcomes-based assessment process. As the primary users of the higher education system, students can provide unique insights throughout the entire process.

In terms of the design of the assessment process, it is important to establish a clear timeline for the development of the assessment plan itself as well as how long the actual assessment process (e.g., data collection, analysis, and use of results) will take. The assessment plan should include a clear purpose related to the mission, goals, program objectives, and learning outcomes of the institution as a whole, and of the student affairs office. Chapter 3 examines each of the components of the assessment process in greater detail. Other considerations include determining who will carry out the assessment and what instruments will be used, as well as deciding how to collect, analyze, and disseminate the information yielded by the assessment instrument. We offer insights about involving stakeholders in the assessment process and how to engage in effective outcomes-based assessment in chapters 5 and 6.

Ultimately, outcomes-based assessment is not just about garnering the results and disseminating the information but using those results to understand and enhance student learning and development (Banta, 2004; Banta & Associates, 2002; Bresciani, 2006; Maki, 2004; Palomba & Banta, 1999; Schuh, et al., 2001; Upcraft & Schuh, 1996). Chapter 5 addresses these issues in detail.

Because institutional environments may differ widely from campus to campus, there are several ways to use the results of assessment. In other words, there is no one right answer. It is, therefore, important for student affairs professionals to consider the culture of their institutions when using assessment results. Kuh, Gonyea, and Rodriguez (2002) argue that the results may provide a rationale for programs, services, and initiatives as well as highlight particular policies, programs, and practices in need of review. Palomba and Banta (1999) concur by describing the many ways assessment results may be used for daily tasks such as planning, budgeting, teaching, and learning. Each of these areas is discussed in further detail in chapters 5 and 6.

Evaluation and Research

Now that we have defined what assessment is, it is necessary to explain how it is different from other commonly used terms, including *evaluation* and *research*. Schuh and Upcraft (1999) argue that evaluation is linked to but should be differentiated from assessment. The authors also assert that "evaluation is any effort to use assessment evidence to improve departmental, divisional, or institutional effectiveness" (p. 19). Many professionals stop the inquiry process at the data collection and analysis phase and fail to communicate the results. This not only leaves institutional stakeholders in the dark in terms of those activities and experiences that contribute to or hinder student learning, it also impedes the ability to improve programs and services because the pertinent information is not shared. Palomba and Banta (1999) support this argument when they assert that assessment must be "shared and used in meaningful ways" to be of use to an institution (p. 297). Evaluation is the means by which assessment results may be used in meaningful ways.

Research and assessment, according to Erwin (1991), have many similarities but are differentiated in two primary ways. The first difference, explained by Schuh and Upcraft (1999), is that assessment informs practice, and research informs the development of theories and challenges or tests ideas.

The second difference focuses on the implications of the two concepts. The results of assessment are generally only applicable to an individual institution or to a specific practice or process within an institution. On the other hand, if conducted with sound methodology, research is generally broad in its implications for student affairs and higher education in general and is not institution specific (Upcraft & Sohuh, 1996). Although not directly tied to assessment, research may be used in the process of developing learning outcomes or designing the experiences that are intended to deliver the desired outcomes. For example, a unit in the Division of Student Affairs may base learning outcomes on a particular student development theory that was devised from research about a particular type of college student. Research may also be used to help interpret the application of the findings. However, programmatic outcomes-based assessment may rarely follow strict research methodology. While institutional outcomes-based assessment may follow strict research methodology, the findings may still not be generalizable.

The point in all this is to clarify that outcomes-based assessment is not intended to be research. Outcomes-based assessment was designed to be a systematic, self-reflection process that provides the practitioner with information on how to improve his or her planning and delivery processes. While findings from this process are most likely not generalizable in other settings, the data gathered can be instrumental in demonstrating accountability for the program as well as the institution (Bresciani, 2009).

When considering the comparison of outcomes-based assessment to research in the implementation of outcomes-based assessment, outcomes-based assessment is not used to "prove" that learning and development are occurring. Rather, outcomes-based assessment embraces Papert's (1991) epistemology of situational constructionist learning. In this epistemology, the notion of discovery and response to that discovery is paramount. In other words, Papert suggests that the more we learn about how well we are delivering or explaining what we hope students will be able to know and do in a certain situation, the more we will refine our delivery so that we will see more evidence of student learning and development in that specific situation.

In this model, the delivery and improvement of learning is situational: It is situational to what the students know prior to their coming into the classroom, workshop, or training module; it is situational to knowing the teaching strengths of the instructor; and it is situational to the entire environment where the learning opportunity is designed. Furthermore, it is situational to how well the instructors collaborate with one another to plan learning connections from one course to the next and situational to how well instructors integrate learning with opportunities to reinforce that learning outside the classroom, as in the case of cocurricular activities, or how well the learning challenges the individual students or how well individual students are supported by academic support services.

While the implementation of the outcomes-based assessment is situational, it is not void of what research has shown to be effective methods of evaluating learning and development. For example, research shows that the more a student engages in the campus community, the more the student will persist in his or her higher education and the more likely the student will succeed academically (Kuh et al., 2005; Manning, Kinzie, & Schuh, 2006). Given this, instructors and cocurricular professionals might design interventions for their specific students that would contribute to their students' engagement with the academic community. They would evaluate the designed intervention for the portion of engagement that they were able to deliver. This may involve, for example, the student's ability to identify networks of peers he or she could socialize with and seek tutorial assistance from. The professionals would then see a level of detail in the data about how they could actually improve that engagement experience for that student. While they could also evaluate whether the persistence rate increased for that group of students, the persistence rate alone would not tell them anything about how to improve the actual intervention without assessment of the faculty input.

The situational nature of outcomes-based assessment is its strength and its weakness. Its strength lies in the rich collection of data that can inform specific improvements in the way learning occurs, how it is designed, delivered, and evaluated. The data collected from outcomes-based assessment practices inform conversations for real improvement (Allen, 2004; Banta & Associates, 2002; Bresciani, 2006; Bresciani, Zelna, & Anderson, 2004; Maki, 2004; Palomba & Banta, 1999; Suskie, 2004) but need input from all stakeholders. The weakness resides in the reality that the situationally derived data are not generalizable. The nongeneralizability of the data makes across-program and across-institutional comparisons of learning and development difficult. We address how to remedy this challenge in chapter 11.

Types of Assessment

When implementing outcomes-based assessment at any institution it can be helpful to articulate the intended goal(s) of your assessment so that you are able to identify which type can best serve you. While this book focuses on implementing outcomes-based assessment for student success, it is important for us to also include the various other types of assessment. For simplicity's sake, the types of assessment can be divided into five main categories:

1. Needs assessment
2. Utilization assessment
3. Assessment of satisfaction
4. Assessment based on Astin's I-E-O Model
5. Outcomes-based assessment of student learning and development (Bresciani et al., 2004)

Each component except for the assessment of student learning and development is discussed here.

Needs assessment focuses on determining the types of services and programs that students indicate they would like or need. Some of these needs could be drawn, indirectly, from such instruments as the Beginning College Survey of Student Engagement (BCSSE), which looks at what students hope to participate in when they enter college. Other methods of assessment can include those introduced in chapter 4. The important point is that needs assessment is used to determine constituents' desired services and programs as perceived by the constituents included in the assessment process. Needs assessment can be used in the assessment of student learning and development to inform the development of new services (e.g., learning opportunities for students). Or one can simply articulate outcomes for programs and services and determine whether the intended programs and services are desired by the constituents by asking the constituents to comment on the value of those outcomes.

Utilization assessment focuses on the students/constituents who are using your services. Information gathered in utilization assessment can include the number of students using a particular service, the type of student using your service (e.g., differentiating among age, ethnicity, and standing), and details about when the service is employed. Capturing students' use of services can be accomplished through many means including sign-in sheets, identification card swipe systems, and data-gathering software. Utilization information can inform facilities management, personnel workload discussions, and the timing and placement of programs and advertising. In addition, utilization data may be used to help interpret the meaning of results generated from outcomes-based assessment.

Assessment of satisfaction explores students' satisfaction with a particular service or a service entity as a whole. National standardized assessment tools include the Educational Benchmarking Surveys and the Noel-Levitz Satisfaction Survey. Assessment of satisfaction can be an important component of the assessment of student learning and development as students who express higher levels of satisfaction with services at an institution tend to perform at a higher rate (Kuh, Kinzie, Buckley, Bridges, & Hayek, 2006). However, satisfaction surveys on their own do not tell us why students are or are not satisfied. And often the satisfaction surveys do not help us understand the level of specificity about what parts of the program and services they were satisfied with. Therefore, we have no information to improve the programs students are dissatisfied with, nor do we know which parts of our programs and services to keep because we don't know that those pieces are what students are specifically happy about.

Astin's (1991) *I-E-O Model* of assessment provides a framework to examine the inputs (e.g., background characteristics and prior knowledge), environment (e.g., the college experience), and outputs (e.g., knowledge a student possesses upon graduation) associated with a student's transition through college. This assessment approach is associated with a quasi-experimental methodology and thus is most readily measured with pre- and post-test methodology. The pretest will account for a student's knowledge and stage of development upon entering an environment. The student will experience the environment, and the posttest will measure what the student has gained through participating in that environment while accounting for the student's initial inputs. This is the most sophisticated assessment approach as it intends to measure the value-added of the experience the student is engaged in. It is also the most time-consuming. To be implemented well, Astin's I-E-O requires attention to sampling and other variables that may influence the measurement of the experience.

Importance of Outcomes-Based Assessment in Student Affairs Work

American higher education is in the throes of one of the most challenging times in history. Increasing demands for accountability for student learning by internal and external stakeholders, ever-decreasing resources, eroding public confidence, and greater numbers of students from diverse backgrounds going to college than ever before present many challenges to those responsible for creating meaningful and inspiring cocurricular learning environments. The quality and extent of learning taking place at the collegiate level is under intense scrutiny, and assessment is a primary way to "operationalize our notions about excellence" (Astin, 1991, p. 5).

In the past, faculty members were primarily responsible for demonstrating student learning on college and university campuses. Today a greater understanding of the value and impact of the out-of-class experience on overall student learning and development, and the need for student affairs professionals to justify the existence of their programs and services in a time of diminishing resources, call for effective assessment of the out-of-class learning experience. According to the Student Learning Imperative (SLI; American College Personnel Association [ACPA], 1994), student affairs work has a dual purpose: to complement and enhance the mission of the institution while encouraging and assisting with student learning and personal development. Student learning and development in turn are inextricably intertwined and serve as the primary focus of outcomes-based assessment in student affairs.

The ACPA and National Association for Student Personnel Administrators (NASPA) (2004) further the notions of the SLI in their joint document *Learning Reconsidered*. According to the authors of this document, student affairs work "is integral to the learning process because of the opportunities it provides students to learn through action, contemplation, reflection, and emotional engagement as well as information acquisition" (p. 12). Moreover, in their work about creating educationally effective environments, Kuh et al. (2005) assert that the activities students are engaged in during their postsecondary experience have a greater impact on their learning than their background characteristics or the specific institution they attend. The authors also summarize the two primary components of student engagement that contribute to overall student success in college. The amount of time expended and effort exerted by students in academic and cocurricular pursuits is the first component. The second is how a college or university allocates resources and organizes learning-centered experiences and services that are of interest and of benefit to students (Kuh et al., 2005). Outcomes-based assessment acts as a valuable tool for those working to enhance student engagement by informing resource allocations and shedding light on those activities that students are not only interested in but also readily participate in and learn from.

The degree to which student affairs affects learning at a particular college or university may vary from department to department or program to program. The importance of the contribution of outcomes-based assessment of student learning in student affairs may be summarized by these four categories:

- accountability
- resources and funding
- planning, policy, and programming
- creating a culture of continuous improvement

Accountability for Student Learning and Development

According to Donald and Denison (2001), the public demand for accountability in higher education has increased progressively since the beginning of the 1990s. This phenomenon is echoed and discussed throughout much of the higher education assessment literature of the past decade (Bresciani, 2006; Palomba & Banta, 1999; Schuh et al., 2001; Upcraft & Schuh, 1996). Increases in tuition and fees not matched by financial aid offerings, college graduates with limited ability to compete in the national and global marketplace, and growing dissatisfaction with the quality of classroom instruction are just a few of the factors contributing to the public disenchantment with the higher education enterprise (Bresciani; Palomba & Banta; Schuh et al.; Upcraft & Schuh).

Bresciani (2006) asserts that the intention behind outcomes-based assessment is "that of quality assurance and external accountability" (p. 13). Palomba and Banta (1999) parallel this notion by explaining that assessment is key for improving the quality of educational programs as well as for building trust with external and internal stakeholders. In recent years federal and state governments have increased demands for accountability in postsecondary education (Burke, 2005). Student affairs professionals in particular are faced with the often daunting task of demonstrating the impact of their work on overall student learning and development. Outcomes-based assessment, when undertaken effectively, yields tangible results that clearly demonstrate where and how learning is facilitated and enhanced in the cocurricular collegiate environment.

In addition to increasing levels of scrutiny by stakeholders and the state and federal governments, assessment is now a key component of the accreditation process. According to Ewell (2005), the new accrediting requirements of the early 1990s asked that institutions develop learning outcomes, create and use assessment tools, and use the results to improve programs and services. Much of the focus of the accreditation process historically focused on the classroom. In recent years, however, a shift toward considering the in-class and out-of-class learning environment has resulted in more of a holistic look at student learning and development. As a result, in the words of Upcraft and Schuh (1996), assessment has moved from "the 'nice to have if you can afford it' category to the 'you better have it if you want to get accredited' category" (p. 7).

On a final note, it is important to differentiate between accountability and outcomes-based assessment. Accountability is a call by external, and sometimes internal, stakeholders for higher education institutions to demonstrate that they are not just graduating students, but that they are actually producing and encouraging the learning they claim. Additionally, accountability demands that institutions demonstrate they are effectively using resources and contributing to the overall growth and development of their students. Outcomes-based assessment provides a means for assessing the levels and types of learning that occur. It is a tool or process that is intentional in nature and helps guide the development of programs and services, and thus it serves the purpose of accountability.

However, since outcomes-based assessment of particular programs may not use methods that result in comparable findings, those external to higher education who cry out for accountability may not readily recognize the value of the formative assessment processes that are in place to improve programs. So it is important for the student affairs professional to determine where he or she desires to engage in institutional assessment that will produce comparable results or in programmatic assessment that will produce data that drive decision making to improve specific programs and differentiate between them. More details on this are in chapters 7, 9, and 11.

Resources and Funding to Improve Student Learning and Development

The strong impetus for outcomes-based assessment of student affairs work is the desire to demonstrate necessity and value in a time of decreasing resources (Palomba & Banta, 1999; Upcraft & Schuh, 1996). Among student affairs professionals there is little dissention about the significant role that student affairs professionals' work plays in student learning and development. However, decision-making bodies at institutions of higher education may not be aware of the contribution student affairs programs and services have on student learning and may allocate resources according to "narrowly defined academic priorities" (Upcraft & Schuh, p. 8).

Outcomes-based assessment provides a vehicle for demonstrating the vital role student affairs plays in facilitating student learning and development. In addition to gauging affordability and the cost-effectiveness of programs and services, student affairs professionals may use outcomes-based assessment to demonstrate their commitment and contributions to the academic mission of their institutions (Upcraft & Schuh, 1996). They may also use the process to manage expectations for what can truly be accomplished given particular organizational structures, resource allocations, and time committed to specific intervention and developmental activities (Bresciani, 2006). Outcomes-based assessment results inform the rationale for the continuation of current, and the development of new, cocurricular programs and services and may be used to demonstrate how financial and human capital are used to enhance student learning and development. Recommendations derived from results may encourage conversations and collaborations across divisional lines, all resulting in the improvement of student success.

Planning, Policy, and Programming

The SLI (ACPA, 1994) suggests that effective and enriching student affairs policies and programs should stem from research on student learning and institutional assessment data. Student learning research provides a general knowledge base to draw conclusions and to gain insight for decision making, programming, and planning. Institution-specific assessment data provide information about institutional culture and context and their impact on how policies, procedures, and programs are implemented on a particular college or university campus. Combining research and assessment data provides a comprehensive foundation of information that may be used to inform policy making and develop meaningful, learning-centered programming.

Upcraft and Schuh (1996) assert that assessment can assist student affairs professionals with decisions regarding the type and scope of programs and services as well as yield information about how much student learning results from a particular service or initiative. With regard to strategic planning, assessment helps identify goals and objectives and highlights any issues in need of resolution before such goals and objections are realized (Upcraft & Schuh). Assessment data yield information about potential strengths and weaknesses in planning, programming, and policy making and provide a systematic means for effective decision making. Such data may also inform strategic planning efforts by helping create priorities through identifying areas that are performing well or in need of improvement, or by considering action plans created and used by any number of student affairs departments as a result of their assessment activities. It is, demonstrably, a very useful component of departmental, divisional, and institutional program review. By using the results of assessment in developing programs, services, and policies, student affairs professionals can ensure student learning remains at the core of their work.

Astin (1991) argues that "an institution's assessment practices are a reflection of its values" (p. 3). He goes on to say, "Assessment practices should further the basic aims and purposes of our higher education institutions" (p. 3). Student learning and development are at the center of any college or university mission and, therefore, serve as the guiding principles of the majority of academic and student affairs work. To ascertain whether student learning takes place as a result of the programs and services provided by student affairs professionals, it is necessary to consult the results of the institution-specific outcomes-based assessment report.

Culture of Continuous Improvement for Increased Student Success

Finally, outcomes-based assessment informs and encourages a culture of continuous improvement of student success initiatives and, perhaps more importantly, contributes to the development and maintenance of what Senge (1990) introduced as *learning organizations*. In this type of organization, the members have a commitment to shared learning and continuous discourse. Assumptions, values, and ways of doing and knowing are routinely reviewed and often challenged, and collaboration within and between organizational departments or groups enables the implementation of new and innovative approaches to student learning and development.

According to Maki (2004), "An institutional commitment to assessing for learning builds over time as a campus or system learns how to develop, integrate, or adapt practices, structures, processes, and channels of communication that support and value a collective commitment to institutional learning" (p. 172). It is important, therefore, that student affairs professionals actively embrace a culture of outcomes-based assessment and work together over time to develop a meaningful and systematic process in which important stakeholders are engaged so that efforts to improve student success become systematic, pervasive, and collaborative.

Researchers all agree that the results of outcomes-based assessment are fruitless if they are not shared with appropriate stakeholders and implemented effectively (Bresciani, 2006; Maki, 2004; Palomba & Banta, 1999; Schuh et al., 2001; Upcraft & Schuh, 1996). The results of outcomes-based assessment may be used either to inform the evaluation of programs and services to highlight general issues hindering student learning or to point toward issues specific to one particular program, type of student, or service, to name just a few. In accordance with the SLI (ACPA, 1994), which states, "Knowledge and understanding are critical to student success and institutional improvement" (¶ 6), outcomes-based assessment yields meaningful data about the contributions of student affairs work to student learning and development. When embraced as a part of the institutional, divisional, and departmental culture, such assessment provides the framework for continuous improvement and acts as a springboard for dynamic student learning initiatives in student affairs work.

PART TWO

EFFECTIVE OUTCOMES-BASED ASSESSMENT

3

COMPONENTS OF AN EFFECTIVE OUTCOMES-BASED ASSESSMENT PLAN AND REPORT

Throughout the previous two chapters, we discussed the evolution and significance of outcomes-based assessment. Although outcomes-based assessment was once considered an idea that would be short-lived, it has emerged as an essential process to demonstrate how well student affairs' practitioners contribute to student learning and development. This chapter discusses the essential components of an effective outcomes-based assessment plan, which are

- mission statements
- goals
- learning and development outcomes
- methods
- results
- decisions and recommendations that are derived from those results (Bresciani, 2006; Bresciani et al., 2004; Palomba & Banta, 1999; Suskie, 2004)

We also discuss other considerations such as establishing a timeline for reviewing learning outcomes.

How Many Assessment Plans Does One Department Need?

This is a common and a very understandable question. In some institutions, many diverse programs may be organized under one department, or one departmental coordinator may have a variety of roles and responsibilities. In such a situation, how does the department director determine how many assessment plans to write? As is the answer to many questions about outcomes-based assessment, it all depends on what makes the most sense to the professionals who will be using the data derived from the assessment process.

For example, if the student union director manages individuals who primarily take care of facilities management and events planning as well as individuals who are primarily responsible for student life and leadership development, it may make the most sense to draft two initially different assessment plans: one that evaluates outcomes associated with facility usage and customer responsiveness, and one that evaluates outcomes linked to student learning and development in student life and student programs. In addition, imagine that the student life program is quite diverse, including a program that is responsible for disseminating funds to students for a variety of student activities, one that delivers a fairly sophisticated student leadership development program, another that organizes community service, and finally one that assists students with advocacy of student rights. This may mean that rather than creating two assessment plans the department may further break down its student life assessment plan into four to account for the varied learning outcomes of its four programmatic areas. On the other hand, since there is only one individual coordinating all these areas, he or she may decide to have one assessment plan and focus on measuring only the common outcomes shared by all four programs. The approach that is best for this one department is the approach that gives the professionals the most meaningful reflection process necessary to make decisions for continuous improvement. Professionals should have the flexibility to choose between one large assessment plan that evaluates shared outcomes or several plans that focus on evaluating the outcomes that are specific to the programs themselves.

It is important to note that whatever the initial choice may be, the process is iterative and dynamic. This means that while a unit may begin with formulating one assessment plan of common outcomes, over time it may evolve to an assessment plan for each program. The important concept to keep in mind is to plan assessment in the manner that it will be most meaningful and manageable.

Defining Your Mission

When implementing outcomes-based assessment at any institution, it is important to begin with a shared purpose and vision to provide everyone involved in assessment with ownership of the process (Bresciani et al., 2004; Maki, 2004; Palomba & Banta, 1999). By creating a feeling of ownership, faculty, administration, and student affairs practitioners feel vested in the assessment effort and can visibly see how they contribute to the overall process. Student affairs professionals at Frederick Community College found that incorporating learning centeredness in the institution's mission statement allowed them to wholeheartedly embrace assessment (Bresciani et al., 2009). At Isothermal Community College, the department mission statement "was brainstormed in staff meetings" (Bresciani et al., 2009) to allow everyone to include his or her insight on his or her institution's focus on student learning. This collaborative brainstorming provided members of the department with ownership of the department mission and, subsequently, the assessment process. Officials at Sacramento State found that an important part of implementing outcomes-based assessment involved "writing (and subsequently revising, if necessary) a departmental mission statement that is directly aligned with the missions of the University and the Division [of Student Affairs]" (Bresciani, 2009). This alignment between the university and division is discussed in more detail on pp. 33–36 in this chapter.

While all departments or programs within departments may not have mission statements, it will help practitioners focus their programmatic goals if they can, at the very least, derive a shared statement of purpose. So, referring to the example in the first section of this chapter, if a department chooses to have two to six assessment plans, each functional area within the department might not have its own mission statement but will most likely be able to describe the core of its purpose in one or two sentences. Drafting the purpose of the functional area helps focus the drafting of the assessment plan, as it helps the professionals keep in mind the reason the program exists, which may help the professionals remain focused as they articulate the intended end results (e.g., outcomes) of the program.

Defining Goals

When drafting the goals for your division or a department in your division, it is important to define the difference between a *goal* and a *learning outcome*, as the two are often confused. Some programs use *goals* and *objectives* interchangeably; others refer to *outcomes* and *objectives*. Some refer to *institutional goals* when they really intend to be discussing *learning domains*. Others adopt the meaning of the term *outcome* for the term *goal*. It does not necessarily matter what you call any component of the assessment plan as long as there is an institutionally agreed-upon, or at the very least a divisionally agreed-upon, definition for each term.

Goals are typically known to be broad statements that can often be incorporated as part of the strategic plan for the division (Bresciani et al., 2004). These are not measured/identified by one outcome but rather they are measured/identified through a combination of many learning outcomes that are derived from the goals. Student affairs professionals at California State University Sacramento reiterate this when they state that

> planning goals are seen as broad statements that describe the overarching, long-range intentions of an administrative unit. As such, they are used primarily for general planning, as starting points for the development and refinement of program objectives or student learning outcomes. (Bresciani et al., p. 112)

The articulation of goals often incorporates the professional's values. The goals may be quite ambitious, and that is fine, as they are not directly measurable. In writing programmatic goals professionals often are able to express the values that inspire their work. This is where we write about our aspirations to change student behavior and to transform students' lives. For example, staff at Frederick Community College Student Life wrote the goal: "Students will become self-directed learners by developing personal, organizational and community awareness and will strengthen communication, interpersonal, and critical-thinking/problem solving skills" (Bresciani et al., in press). An Oregon State University goal is that "students build connections between their University curriculum, co-curriculum and career goals."

Learning outcomes, in contrast, are very detailed and examine a particular competency that we hope students will accomplish. Many methods of assessment (e.g., case studies, pre- and posttests, surveys) can be used to assess one particular learning outcome. Therefore, many outcomes and many assessment methods may be specified for one goal.

While pondering the values and goals of the student affairs division and/or departments in that division, it is important to remember that the university operates as one unit in the development of the whole student and that academic affairs and student affairs serve to complement each other. As such, it is beneficial to align unit goals to university-wide goals, if the relationship of goals is noted in the division's assessment plan(s). Officials at Northern Arizona University found it important to "develop assessment goals that align[ed] with divisional and university goals" (Bresciani et al., in press). Staff at John Carroll University recognized that

> the development of the strategic goals was an iterative and inclusive process, taking place over several months with the participation of multiple representatives from each department and from different levels of responsibility. By involving so many people from a variety of areas, they are able to understand the foundational role of assessment in the strategic plan and, more importantly, align their departmental initiatives and assessment projects with the divisional goals. (Bresciani et al.)

By displaying the relationship of unit goals with department, division, and university-wide goals, all stakeholders can be assured that they are demonstrating a shared commitment to embracing student learning and that they are in communication with each other about what the institutional values should be. Officials of student affairs divisions who adopt learning goals in isolation of their academic colleagues are not necessarily demonstrating the collaborative learning framework that outcomes-based assessment is intended to promote. While many helpful resources exist to stimulate ideas for what divisional learning outcomes can be, such as those publications from the Council on the Advancement of Standards, ACPA, and NASPA, developing outcomes in isolation of your institution's learning outcomes, or at the very least institutional general education outcomes, is not reinforcing the essence of cocurricular learning and the collaborative design of curriculum. In other words, if you do not work collaboratively with your academic colleagues to articulate shared learning outcomes that they have designed in their curriculum, or at least simply map your outcomes to their general education outcomes, you are creating an isolated institutional learning outcomes conversation, which defeats the very purpose of assessing student learning and development in the cocurriculum.

Distinguishing Between Types of Learning Outcomes

Before drafting learning outcomes, it is important to distinguish between the different types of learning outcomes: institutional, divisional, and programmatic. Institutional learning outcomes refer to what institutional leadership expects all students, regardless of discipline, to be able to know and do upon graduation. These are often quite broad as they refer to the entire collegiate experience. For example, institutional leadership may want its students to be globally competent citizens upon graduation. An institution may also opt to have divisional-level learning outcomes. If an institution has divisional outcomes, because of their breadth they will most likely be formulated as goals and not measurable outcomes. However, programmatic learning outcomes will be more specific than institutional outcomes. For example, a programmatic-level learning outcome may state that students will demonstrate multicultural awareness through an articulation of their own personal beliefs and identification of the values and beliefs of others. In this example, the program may be borrowing from the division or institutional goal of multicultural awareness but illustrate the specificity of how multicultural awareness is designed and delivered in the particular program.

Institutional and divisional goals/outcomes are often quite broad, so although they are developed at the institutional or divisional level, they are operationalized and assessed at the department and program levels. If data for the institutional- and divisional-level goals/outcomes are gathered at the institutional or divisional level, the data gathered are often comparative because they are not tied to the actual manner the outcome is delivered; therefore, they are not situationally constructed data. These data can be used in benchmarking and, if gathered with sound methodology and sampling, the findings may also be considered generalizable to the division, or possibly the institution. While the data gathered at these levels may be comparable, the findings rarely lead to the types of decisions necessary to improve programs. Findings may reveal where more refined assessment is needed in a program, but findings typically do not inform detailed decisions that will improve programmatic offerings.

Department and programmatic outcomes are much more specific than institutional or divisional learning outcomes as they are written in a format that allows them to be identified in the particular situation in which they are delivered. The data gathered to measure specifically worded outcomes will also allow for decisions to be made for improvement in the department or a particular program. Department- and program-level outcomes, because of the smaller populations, the specificity of the outcomes, and the way the learning is situationally constructed, are not generalizable to a larger population.

Drafting Learning Outcomes

Although each of the previously stated levels of learning outcomes may not be present on every campus, it is important to recognize and value the degree to which each and every thing we do on campus influences student learning and development, and to keep this in mind when we are designing new programs. It is important to consider the big picture of how we contribute to the university mission and how we can better prepare our students to enter the workforce upon graduation. This section explains how to draft quality learning-outcome statements.

Drafting quality, robust learning-outcome statements is an essential part of the assessment plan, as everything else in the plan is derived from these statements. As already noted, while there are other types of assessment that focus on matters such as identifying student needs, use of facilities, student satisfaction, and the evaluation of the services themselves, this book's focus is on learning and development outcomes. These other types of assessment, discussed in chapter 2, are each valuable. They can inform the formulation, interpretation, and evaluation of learning outcomes. As such, they are important components of the outcomes-based assessment process. Yet, on their own these types of assessment practices do not directly evaluate your program's contribution to students' behavior, cognitive abilities, or affective behaviors. Learning and development outcome statements focus on the "knowledge, skills, attitudes, and habits of mind" (Suskie, 2004, p. 75) that students gain from participating in a program or activity. This essentially refers to what students demonstrate they know or are able to do upon completion of a workshop, an activity, or a series of workshops.

Some student affairs practitioners have challenges with articulating outcomes because they have trouble differentiating outcomes from the goals they have for their students and the actual ability they have to influence those goals (Bresciani, in press-c). For example, most student affairs practitioners enter the profession because they desire to change students' lives. The student affairs professionals want to see students become self-actualized, become responsible citizens, take responsibility for their decisions, or engage in wellness behaviors.

While these goals inspire the practitioners to work the number of hours they do, they are indeed goals and not necessarily direct outcomes of the day-to-day work. No one can take away the goals and dreams we have for our students, yet if we want to try to influence those goals, we need to purposefully design and evaluate programs that will shape the fruition of these goals. To do so, we need to design and evaluate programs that lead the student to choose to change his or her own behavior. This means that our programs must be designed to provide students with the opportunity to learn the knowledge, skills, and possibly the attitudes that lead to behavior change (Banta, 2004).

Bresciani et al. (2004) identified three criteria to consider when drafting learning outcomes. These criteria include creating measurable, meaningful, and manageable outcome statements. The following is a list of questions, adapted from Bresciani et al., concerning the criteria to consider when drafting a learning outcome:

- Is it measurable, meaning is it identifiable, not necessarily countable?
- Is it meaningful to the organization and the students it serves? Does this outcome represent a priority for our organization?
- Is it manageable? Do we really have the means to deliver and evaluate the intended outcome?
- From whom will I be gathering evidence to know that my outcome has been met? Can I readily access that population when I need to?
- Who would know if my outcome has been met? Who else can help me identify the criteria to evaluate the outcome? Or whom can I collaborate with to evaluate the outcome? Who possibly shares this outcome?
- How will I know if it has been met? What does meeting the outcome look like? Can I determine if the outcome has been met while I have the students within my locus of control?
- Will it provide me with evidence that will lead me to make a decision for continuous improvement? Am I evaluating an outcome that has more than a yes or no answer? How will evaluating this outcome help me inform a decision or a recommendation to improve the overall program?

When examining a learning outcome, the reader should be able to identify what is being measured (What is it that you want the student to have gained from all the activity you planned?), and it should be clear how that knowledge or skill will be demonstrated. Often the use of active verbs can help clarify exactly what it is that students are expected to know or be able to do (Suskie, 2004). For example, administrators at John Carroll University say that students will be able to "articulate the role of Jesuit identity and mission in their work as student leaders" (Bresciani et al., in press). This learning outcome will be demonstrated by students actually identifying, either orally or in writing, the role that their Jesuit identity has played in their work in leadership positions. The action word *articulate* allows us to measure an end result that we can visibly observe. As John Carroll is a religious institution, Jesuit identity is a concept that is heavily valued. As previously mentioned, it is important to connect outcomes with values, as the values are what drive the planning and implementation of programs, and therefore values drive their assessment. This outcome statement also identifies (a) what the students should have gained and (b) how the competency will be demonstrated.

The use of Bloom's Taxonomy tools (for example, those retrieved from Web sites such as http://www.coun.uvic.ca/learn/program/hndouts/bloom .html) allows practitioners to determine what level of learning is reasonable for the student given the opportunity provided to the learner. For example, you would not expect a student to demonstrate a high-level learning outcome if you only have 1 hour in a workshop with a student. A 2-hour workshop or a 3-day retreat is unlikely to make students globally competent; however, students may be able to identify their values during such an event. Therefore, a learning outcome for students at a 3-day leadership retreat may read something like: Students will articulate their personal values and beliefs and how these beliefs may have an impact on their leadership role on campus. Thus, as you draft your outcomes, you may want to pay particular attention to the opportunity you have provided the student to learn what you expect the student to be able to learn. Action verbs indicating a lower-level learning are appropriate for brief learning opportunities while higher-level learning action verbs can be used when there are consistent, longer-term learning opportunities provided to a student.

In addition to being mindful of the level of learning that can be expected from students, given the opportunity provided to them to learn, consider whether the use of outcomes that infer pre- and posttest design is worth the time and effort that pre- and posttest assessment requires. In other words, when writing outcomes that include active verbs such as *improve, increase,* or *gain,* determine whether you really need to show the value added of one program. Doing so creates an inordinate amount of work that may simply not be necessary. Rather, you may want to select action verbs that indicate clearly to the student what you expect him or her to do to demonstrate the learning and development you expect from your well-designed program.

It is beneficial to the student and practitioner if the learning and development outcomes are based on the theories that undergird the practice, which provides opportunities for students to learn them (Bresciani, 2009). Administrators at Texas A&M University encourage the use of theories when practitioners are formulating outcomes and methods of assessment.

Some of the outcomes are now based on a single theory/model, and others are a combination of several congruent theories and models. Subcommittees at the university continued to refine their work, and encouragement came from the whole committee to test the rubrics with student leaders and student organizations (Bresciani et al., in press).

However, sometimes practitioners are not cognizant of the theories used in their practice; thus, the outcomes may lack depth. The outcomes become more difficult to evaluate as the criteria for identifying the learning outcomes are simply not known to the one who is doing the evaluating. Bridging the theories of practice to the outcomes and criteria for evaluating that practice is essential to systematic and well-informed decisions for continuous improvement.

Finally, it is important for student affairs practitioners to start evaluating where it makes the most sense for them to do so. Some professionals start with evaluating the outcomes where they believe they have very little to improve; others start by evaluating their problem areas. Others start by evaluating the learning of their paraprofessionals and then move on from there. And still others begin by evaluating the effectiveness of their outreach programs, such as workshops, orientations, and presentations in classrooms. They then move on to evaluating the effectiveness of one-on-one consultations, then on to the effectiveness of informational literature and Web portals.

As the intention of the assessment process is to demonstrate student learning and development, learning outcome statements should measure just that instead of simply measuring student satisfaction. Satisfaction, matriculation, and graduation statistics can be used in the assessment process in combination with other data. These data are often an important component of program and performance reviews and they may be helpful in interpreting why outcomes have or have not been met; however, the purpose of the outcomes-based assessment process is to focus formatively on student learning and development throughout a student's entire college experience instead of simply the end result (e.g., matriculation or graduation statistics).

Mapping Learning Outcomes

As we discuss mapping learning outcomes, we are really talking about an alignment process. Here, we discuss two types of alignment processes. One is the alignment of program learning outcomes to program goals, division goals, institutional goals, or professional standards. The second alignment process involves planning. This is the process where the professionals check to see if they actually have designed an opportunity for the student to learn what they expect the student to learn. This is an alignment of the activities planned with the intended end results (e.g., outcomes).

Mapping program, activity, and department learning outcomes back to department, division, and institutional learning goals helps align unit outcomes with important goals of the division and institution. Such mapping allows higher-level decision makers to identify who intends to meet the division or institutional goals. This is a helpful process particularly when institutions may allocate funding to particular strategic goals and initiatives. In other words, when an institution can identify which programs align intended outcomes with strategic or funding priorities, the institution can tell more quickly how targeted funding is influencing expected improvements in the strategic areas identified.

Officials at Widener University use mapping on many different levels in their student affairs division.

> The experience [of mapping division learning outcomes back to general education outcomes] was informative to staff, since there was significant alignment. The process of mapping general education goals to Student Affairs learning objectives affirmed the significant contributions of student affairs experiences in the learning processes and results. A similar process was used by the staff to map the learning objectives to the institutional learning objectives. (Bresciani et al., 2009)

This mapping will also allow other departments to see where collaboration can occur with programs and activities.

Planning the Delivery of Your Outcomes

After establishing learning outcomes for your unit or department, a next step in the process may be to establish a map of the programs and activities where the learning outcomes will be introduced and reinforced. This will allow you as a professional, and possibly the student as well, to see which activities and programs are specifically designed for students to achieve the intended department outcomes. Maki (2004) describes this as a gridlike document where learning outcomes are introduced, reinforced, or emphasized, and the outcomes are labeled as such. So one particular learning outcome may be introduced in two programs or activities, reinforced in three other department-level activities, and emphasized or evaluated in a different program. Aligning activities planned to meet intended outcomes is an excellent way to ensure that all learning outcomes are met. This process ensures that programs and activities provide opportunities for students to fulfill each learning goal and that no goals are overly emphasized (see Table 1).

Many institutions use this method of mapping learning outcomes because it is quick and efficient in terms of having an overview of learning outcomes and how they are met within the student affairs division. Suskie (2004) details a way to accomplish this mapping by "[creating] a grid listing your institution's or program's major learning goals down the left side and required courses and other curricular requirements across the top" (p. 59). The only adaptation needed for student affairs purposes would be to list department or division outcomes down the side of the grid and the programs or activities where the outcomes will be met across the top. At North Carolina State University, "the staff has been better able to articulate learning outcomes as a result of tying their significant activities back to department level outcomes" (Bresciani et al., 2009).

TABLE 1
Example of a Curriculum Alignment Map for Student Affairs

Outcomes	*Five-minute 1st-year class presentations*	*Workshop*	*First-year experience class session*	*Web site*
Students will be able to explain consequences of violating the honor code				

As professionals ensure that they actually provide students with opportunities to learn the intended outcomes, they may be able to identify means of assessment that naturally occur within the learning opportunity provided to students. On the other hand, they may also need to identify and create a new means or new opportunities to demonstrate the learning in a way that provides feedback that enables systematic improvement. For example, if you are evaluating a learning outcome such as, "Students will be able to explain consequences of violating the honor code," the next question is: How do you provide students with an opportunity to learn this expected outcome?

As you describe the opportunities that you provide the student to learn this outcome (see Table 1), you begin to see where you have the best and most systematic opportunity to evaluate and therefore systematically improve the learning outcome. Table 1 lists all the potential opportunities provided by a program for students to learn an expected outcome. It also provides a map of where the best opportunity to influence systematic improvement may occur and assists you as you evaluate which opportunities best promote improved learning. In the example in Table 1, the most influential opportunity to improve learning depends on your locus of control. In other words, if you cannot influence the content of the 1st-year experience course, but you can influence the content of the workshop, you may want to first evaluate the learning of the students who attend the workshop, and then evaluate the 1st-year experience course. However, keep in mind that you have used a high-level learning action verb in your outcome: *explain*. Given that, it may be inappropriate to expect students to meet this outcome after visiting your Web site and after just a 5-minute class presentation. In providing these learning opportunities, you may need to modify the corresponding learning outcomes such as, "Students will be able to list example consequences of violating the honor code."

As you examine how you plan the opportunities for students to learn, and what it is that you expect them to learn, keep in mind that it may well be worth your time to evaluate only the regular and repeated outreach activities, such as workshops, class presentations, and seminars. You can evaluate your students at each new iteration to gather information that will inform your decisions for improvement. However, if you intend to evaluate one-on-one consultations, you will need to make sure your assessment criteria are systematic enough that they can effectively be used for future evaluation. The same is true of your informational literature.

Here are some guiding principles for selecting which learning opportunities to evaluate:

- Where do I have the greatest opportunity to gather the types of information that will improve my planning for this event the next time I deliver it?
- Where do I have the greatest opportunity to influence systematic improvements in student learning and development?
- Do I intend to repeat this activity next quarter, next semester, or next year so that the data I gather will actually influence decisions to improve it the next time I offer it?
- If I evaluate this activity, will I be gathering data that I can use to improve it in the future? And how many students' learning and development may be influenced as a result of the data gathered from this activity?

Choosing a Method to Assess Each Outcome

Another essential component of the assessment plan involves identifying the method used to gather data. There are basically three primary ways to gather assessment data: qualitative, quantitative, or a combination of the two. It is important to realize that gathering assessment data for programmatic assessment plans does not have to involve research. In other words, there is no set sample size necessary, no set way to evaluate the data, and the findings will, most likely, not be generalizable to a larger population. In programmatic assessment, it is important to gather data that will inform decision making.

In institutional assessment, data are often gathered in a manner that involves more rigor with regard to research methods. In institutional assessment, many assumptions are drawn from the data, and it is important that sound sampling strategies be followed as well as thorough, sound research methodology.

The additional difference between the purposes of institutional outcomes-based assessment data collection and programmatic outcomes-based assessment data collection is that institutional data are often used for comparative purposes. As such, they may not be tied to specific programmatic improvement decisions. In order to interpret the value of institutional data, it is important for program administrators to gather appropriate data that will explain the findings of the institutional data. For example, staff at one university gathered the results of a national standardized engagement survey and compared them to those at peer institutions. The vice chancellor of student affairs was concerned that the institution had lower levels of community engagement than its peer institutions. Had student union administrators not gathered their own outcomes-based assessment data for community engagement, they would not have been able to explain to the vice chancellor that the reason for lower community engagement was that the majority of their students sought community within their church organization rather than their higher education institution. And of those who did seek community in their higher education organization, the findings revealed high levels of student engagement. The data derived from programmatic outcomes-based assessment explained why the comparative institutional-level data were really not a bad finding, even though it initially looked as though they were.

When selecting which method(s) of assessment to use when examining your department or program learning outcomes, it is important to realize that multiple methods of assessment will yield more valid results. You may also want to consider how the data will be gathered (e.g., surveys, focus groups, a series of questions after an event) and at which program or activity you can use which method of assessment. We encourage the methods of assessment for each learning outcome to be clearly stated in your assessment plan. Specific methods for assessment are discussed in more depth in chapter 4.

Reporting and Interpreting Results

Reporting the results of the assessment process is of vital importance as this allows you and your colleagues to see how well students are achieving the established outcomes for the department or division and how improvements can be made to help students achieve these outcomes. Reporting the results of assessment can at times be very frustrating. This frustration can stem from the need to keep the results succinct for supervisors and administrators and at the same time from having so much data that it becomes difficult to deem which results are most important and valuable. When you reach this stage, you should consider the intended audience(s) and their expectations (Suskie, 2004; Upcraft & Schuh, 1996). Although you may feel that all your assessment results are valuable, other stakeholders will want to see only the results that are interesting and meaningful for their decision-making process (Suskie).

Another potentially frustrating situation is interpreting the results of the assessment process. It may often be beneficial to consult previous research when interpreting your results. You do not have to do the research to demonstrate, for instance, that high levels of student engagement contribute to high levels of academic success. Your role is to evaluate how well your programs that are designed to engage students are actually engaging students. Theories specific to student affairs, as well as other areas of higher education, can help support or help interpret assessment results.

Numerous resources are available to aid the interpretation of results, both in the published literature and in your own institution. These are discussed further in the next chapter, and many resources to assist you in interpreting results are listed in Appendix A.

Using Results to Make Decisions and Recommendations

In the early stages of planning to implement outcomes-based assessment, it is extremely helpful to engage in a collaborative discussion of how the assessment results will be used, answering such questions as

- What is the appropriate communication routing for the recommended decisions?
- How will decisions and recommendations be prioritized, particularly if new or reallocated resources are required?
- Will the results be used in performance evaluations?
- Will the results be rolled into required annual reports or periodic program reviews?
- How will the results inform strategic planning initiatives?
- With whom will the results be shared within the student affairs division, with the students, faculty members, parents, academic departments, other constituents?

The recommendations resulting from these discussions can be documented as a component of the assessment plan, and further edits should be made to the learning outcomes if necessary. Chapter 5 details specific methods of using and sharing the results and recommendations of the assessment process.

Establishing a Timeline

Establishing a timeline is a very important component of an assessment plan. The timeline is a means to set expectations within the division about when different learning outcomes will be assessed. A timeline may also be established for the implementation of the entire assessment process. It is a good idea to start small with just a few learning outcomes per year and then develop a multiyear assessment plan that evaluates not necessarily everything you do but your key priorities. In your divisional assessment plan (e.g., the plan to evaluate how well your division is engaged in the evidence-based decision-making culture), it is important to indicate how long you expect it will take for all the individual departments within the division to have a fully operational assessment plan with an established set of learning outcomes.

When detailing the timeline for individual unit learning outcomes, it bears repeating that division administrators should keep in mind that it is not necessary for all learning outcomes to be assessed all at once (Bresciani et al., 2004). This task would be overwhelming for any individual. Evaluating one to three learning outcomes at a time will permit each outcome to be examined in depth. After making recommendations based on the results of the initial assessment process, we encourage you to review the timeline detailing when each outcome will be assessed again, to demonstrate that assessment is a continuous process. Recall that each outcome does not have to be assessed every year, but it should be reassessed at an appropriate interval. It is essential to determine whether the decision made to improve student learning and development did indeed improve student learning and development. Such a process creates a built-in internal quality control for decision making and for the quality and integrity of the assessment process.

At Widener University, "reporting mechanisms and timelines were established to allow for regular reporting out to the full staff and to other constituencies" (Bresciani et al., in press) as well. Establishing timelines for the entire assessment process, individual learning outcomes, recommendation implementations, and reporting processes are each essential components of outcomes-based assessment.

Other Components to Be Considered

As each institution is unique, many choose to include additional components in their assessment plans. One such component is to designate the individual responsible for assessing the specific outcomes. In Oregon State University's student affairs assessment plans, a column in the plan is dedicated to naming this person (Bresciani et al., 2009). At North Carolina State University,

> every unit must list the two outcomes to be measured in the upcoming year and articulate the timeline for implementation, intended assessment method (survey, interview, and focus group), and the name of the person or position responsible for the assessment for each outcome. (Bresciani et al.)

After evaluating the learning outcomes you have stated and after identifying the intended improvements you hope to make, you may want to consider incorporating an action plan for the recommendations in your assessment plan or report. Including the budget required to implement the identified improvements may also be valuable. Including such a budget helps with decisions about whether the level of improvement expected from the implementation plan may be worth the investment.

For example, your assessment findings reported that 74% of the students who participated in intramural activities last year demonstrated good sportsmanship after having also participated in four required 1-hour workshops throughout the year. Your recommendation is that if you add two more workshops at a cost of $150 per workshop, you could probably improve the results. When the leadership team of the division evaluates the requests for reallocation of resources and yours is one of them, the leadership team may determine that 74% is just fine. Thus, if you want to make this type of learning improvement in your own department, you will need to identify how to reallocate resources to make it happen.

Thus, other components to consider including in your plan are the comments from upper-level decision makers on whether your recommendations and/or budget requests for improvement should be granted. An explanation of why the recommendation requests were granted or not granted may also be helpful. Including such comments helps close the loop on some decisions where the outcomes may not be improving yet. For example, "The leadership team has made it clear from their funding decisions that improvement in this area is not a priority." It is also helpful to note in this section whether the outcomes being evaluated were linked to larger institutional or divisional strategic initiatives and priorities. Such documentation further emphasizes the linkage or lack thereof of departmental and programmatic assessment to the realization of institutional and divisional goals and priorities.

4

ASSESSMENT METHODS

Once the student learning outcomes have been determined for your department, division, or institution, it is necessary to decide which assessment methods are best suited for measuring the impact of programs and services on student learning and development as related to these outcomes. This chapter does not specifically discuss how to design these assessment and evaluation methods (e.g., surveys and rubrics); many other publications provide resources and cover individual methods extensively (e.g., Bresciani et al., 2004; Maki, 2004; Schuh & Associates, 2009; Suskie, 2004). Rather, this chapter focuses primarily on defining the scope of your assessment project prior to selecting the method. Specifically, this chapter will highlight the differences and similarities between institutional and programmatic methodology beginning with a section of important considerations regardless of whether your scope of assessment is institutional, divisional, or programmatic. This chapter continues with the descriptions of different types of assessment and highlights the differences between institutional and programmatic assessment methodology. Qualitative and quantitative methodologies are then discussed, and institutional and programmatic examples are given in an effort to provide the reader with tangible examples of tools for use in outcomes-based assessment of student learning. Additionally, triangulation and other ways to validate results are presented. The chapter concludes with a series of recommendations anyone engaging in an outcomes-based assessment process should contemplate after selecting a method and prior to putting it into action to ensure that the most effective methods are chosen.

What to Consider Before Selecting Appropriate Methods

Defining Your Scope

The ideal model for outcomes-based assessment is Astin's (1991) I-E-O Model. The improvement of student success is enhanced greatly when one first considers the inputs (e.g., first-generation college student, family socio-economic status) a student enters the institution with, how the environment (e.g., college experience) affects the student, and the outcomes the student leaves the institution with. To truly understand the value-added experience of a student, student affairs professionals must first understand where students were/are cognitively, affectively, socially, and behaviorally before they participate in a particular program, service, or activity (e.g., experience). The understanding of input data serves as a baseline that informs the interpretation of results (e.g., realized outcomes) gathered from evaluating the student affairs experience. However, gathering this kind of baseline data requires a sophistication of the assessment process and an investment in time that very few institutions have the resources for. Yet it is important for us to maintain the ideal model when considering design of evaluation methods for outcomes-based assessment.

In addition to noting the ideal of Astin's I-E-O Model, it is also necessary to revisit the differences between research and assessment. Assessment, if you recall, is used to inform practice; research is used to inform the development of theories and challenges or to test ideas. Moreover, research is generally much broader in the scope of its implications and is not typically considered institutionally specific. The results of research may be applied in many higher education settings, whereas the results of assessment are typically applicable only to the institutional program where the assessment took place (Schuh & Upcraft, 2001).

Institutional assessment and programmatic assessment are two types of inquiry that are often assumed to be one and the same. When considering methods, it is first necessary to determine the scope of the project at hand. This book focuses on outcomes-based assessment in student affairs, which is different in scope than the broader-based institutional assessment. Methods for each type of assessment do, in fact, differ and it is important to recognize such differences. Institutional assessment typically involves a much larger sample size, and the answers to the questions under investigation are able to be generalized or applied to all students at the institution as long as the methodology and sampling procedures are rigorous; thus, it resembles the methodology more akin to research. This approach differs from programmatic assessment, which is created to discover information that leads to decisions to improve a specific program for a subgroup in the larger student population.

To illustrate the differences between institutional and programmatic assessment, consider the following examples. Staff at an Office of Residence Life might assess the impact of training on the leadership and communication skills of its resident assistants. This is a programmatic assessment because it looks at the impact of one specific program, and the results of such a program assessment are only applicable to those students who are resident assistants and who participated in the training. Now, if the residence life office staff decides to evaluate the community engagement skills of all the students enrolled in the institution to illustrate the intended outcome—that those who reside in residence halls demonstrate higher levels of community engagement than those who do not—a method that uses rigorous sampling and methodology would need to be employed.

Choosing a Method Based on Articulated Outcomes

First, before determining the exact method for use in your outcomes-based assessment process, it is necessary to remember that assessment methods cannot be chosen without first clearly articulating the outcome that you choose to measure (Bresciani et al., 2004). Second, recall that it is important to determine how you deliver the learning experience; there may be a key to selecting the evaluation method in the delivery of the experience. See chapter 3 for more information on writing outcomes and determining the methods to deliver them (e.g., the manner in which students will be able to meet an outcome). Keep in mind that if you select an evaluation method first, without thinking of which outcome the method will be used to measure, you may very well end up with a mound of data that you cannot use, thus wasting valuable resources, especially your time (Bresciani et al., 2004: Suskie, 2004).

Once you have selected your outcome and made sure that you have an opportunity to provide educational experiences that offer the opportunity for the students to attain that outcome, it may be that the opportunity you provide to the student to learn the outcome also becomes the method of evaluation. For example, if you use case studies to teach students about ramifications of violating the student conduct code, you may also be using the discussion of those cases, accompanied by a criteria checklist for the method of evaluation. In this example, the outcome is, "Students will be able to explain ramifications of violations of various aspects of the student conduct code." The method provided to students to learn this is during a 3-hour workshop that is required of students who are reported for first offenses. The students listen to a mini lecture where a checklist is shared about how to determine the ramifications of one's behavior. Then students read aloud sections of the conduct code that spell out the ramifications of their behavior at the university. After this activity, students apply the checklist from the lecture to identify further ramifications beyond university adjudication for their misconduct. Then students are asked to apply what they have gathered from lectures, readings, and discussions to the explanation of what will happen to students in various scenarios/case studies. As the students report the explanations of their particular case study, students listening to the report observe whether their peers have applied all the steps to determining ramifications of their behavior. They do so using the checklist from the lecture; the checklist is their criteria applied to the method of observing the verbal report. The student affairs professional teaching the workshop also applies the checklist to the discussion. While the peers and the professional are using the same method of observation and the same criteria (e.g., checklist), two different lenses are being applied to the evaluation of learning, and as such, those lenses represent, in essence, two types of data collection.

In this example, the student affairs professional took advantage of a naturally occurring opportunity (Ewell, 2003) to evaluate the effectiveness of the learning opportunity. What we mean by this is that the professional used the discussion of the case studies, which served as a peer-teaching tool, as the evaluation method. Naturally occurring methods of assessment often are the most revealing with regard to what can be improved and often are the least time-consuming to evaluate because they are built in to the delivery of the learning. Thus, applying the criteria taught through lecture and reinforced in group discussion, the student affairs professional can easily determine which criteria the students were able to apply and which they were not through observing the student's discussion. As previously mentioned, the student affairs professional has his or her own judgment of student performance in addition to the peer evaluation of the student performance. This provides the professional with two perspectives of data to evaluate to determine exactly what was learned and what was not. In determining what was learned and what was not, the student affairs professional has specific information to improve the design of the workshop as well.

This example emphasizes the importance of first selecting an outcome and making sure you have an opportunity for students to learn that outcome.

As stated in chapter 3, p. 41, the improvement that is most immediate in outcomes-based assessment is when professionals determine whether they even have the means to deliver the intended outcome. In this example, if they were not able to use the case studies as an opportunity to teach the student what they wanted the student to learn, they would not have had the opportunity to use the observation of the case study discussion as the evidence of what was learned. During the process of ensuring that a manner has been provided for the student to actually learn or acquire the outcome that has been identified, student affairs professionals may decide to revise the outcome to fit the method of delivery, or the professionals may realize that they need to completely redesign their way of doing (e.g., the method of delivering the learning) because they forgot to design an opportunity for the student to learn what they intended. We cannot overemphasize enough these first two steps before proceeding further.

Again, as you examine the opportunity that has been designed for the student to realize the intended outcome, you may see a naturally occurring opportunity to evaluate the outcome (Ewell, 2003). If you do not readily identify such an opportunity, then you must design one. For clarification, a naturally occurring opportunity to evaluate student learning resides in the very manner that you had planned to reinforce the learning, such as the case studies in the preceding example. A naturally occurring opportunity is also often known as a *direct* measure of student learning. Direct measures are discussed in greater detail on p. 61. Another example may be that in expecting students to apply conflict resolution skills, you may have designed a role-playing opportunity in which you assign conflict roles to two resident advisers, while the third resident adviser, unaware of the role assignment, must apply conflict resolution skills. The role-playing exercise was designed to reinforce the learning from lectures, readings, and discussions, but it can also serve as the evaluation tool using observation and the criteria that were taught in lecture. Peers and the trainer can evaluate the student's learning by applying the criteria through observation to the role-playing exercise.

If the evaluation method needs to be designed, then it is helpful to identify the type of methodological approach you would like to take. Your choices can include selecting qualitative or quantitative methods. Or you might also choose to employ a mixed-methods approach, which often yields a greater depth of information than either method on its own. As we discuss these methods, keep in mind that we are discussing the application of research methodologies to outcomes-based assessment of programs; therefore, the rigor that would be employed with these methods when used in research is not as apparent when applying them in outcomes-based assessment.

Identifying Appropriate Methods

Maki asserts that the methods one employs to measure student learning should allow for systematic engagement "in critical daily inquiry about discovering what works well and what needs to be improved" (as cited in Bresciani, 2006, p. 15). Moreover, it is important that the methods chosen have meaning to those engaged in the data collection process. This will promote buying into the process to ensure that everyone involved understands how to go about effectively engaging in data collection; to create a common language for the process; and, most importantly, to ensure that data are collected that will inform decisions on how to improve what is being evaluated (Bresciani, 2006).

The methods used for data collection in any assessment project may vary depending on the scope and nature of the issue, the stakeholders involved, and the resources available. Pike (2002) states, "Good research involves asking good questions, and good research questions are both interesting and important" (p. 132). For practitioners engaging in outcomes-based assessment, that means creating outcomes (e.g., research questions) that are directly linked to the mission and goals of the organization, as those are at the core of the institution and naturally embody student learning and development. For example, outcomes-based assessment activity that intends to result in improvement of programs often occurs at the departmental level. It is therefore imperative for a department to develop goals and outcomes for assessment of student learning that are in line with the mission and goals of that department's college or university (Pike, 2002). This will enable the development of interesting outcomes that are directly linked with ideas and objectives that matter in a particular institutional context and culture. When engaging in assessment, one must formulate outcomes that are meaningful and interesting to stakeholders, which may include the students and possibly your faculty colleagues. Additionally, such outcomes must be reasonable and able to be identified, or at least thoroughly investigated, with the time and resources available.

Once the outcomes are determined, appropriate data collection methods can be identified. At this point, according to Pike (2002), those engaged in the assessment process have a plethora of choices to determine the best methods for the assessment project at hand. Will learning be measured at a single point in time (cross-sectional), or will many points in time be used for measuring learning (longitudinal)? Would it be of interest to use the results to make generalizations about a larger population (e.g., institutional assessment) or to focus solely on the individuals studied (e.g., programmatic assessment)? Will the inquiry be qualitative in nature with more reliance on rich, descriptive words than numbers, or quantitative in nature? In regard to the last question, what types of qualitative and quantitative design will be employed, or will the two be used in combination (Pike, 2002)?

Institutional Assessment Methods

When engaging in institutional assessment, it is imperative that validity and reliability are ensured. Reliable assessment measures produce the same results over time, while valid measures use instruments and tools that are appropriate for the task at hand (Creswell, 1998; Denzin & Lincoln, 2000; Palomba & Banta, 1999; Patton, 2002). Nationally recognized and circulated assessment tools, such as the College Student Survey (CSS), the National Survey of Student Engagement (NSSE), and the College Student Experiences Questionnaire (CSEQ), are designed to be reliable and valid. These are tools that can be used with little worry over their rigor, validity, and reliability. Locally developed instruments, however, may require the attention and expertise of those on your college or university campus who are familiar with research and instrument design to ensure the development of valid and reliable instruments.

Benchmarking

Along a similar line of thinking, we must draw attention to the fact that benchmarking or any comparative use of performance indicators is not necessarily considered outcomes-based assessment of student learning and development. Likewise, the methods used for benchmarking differ from those used for outcomes-based assessment. Benchmarking is used for comparison purposes and is generally not geared to identifying or informing programmatic outcomes-based improvements of student learning. Many institutions, for example, may use a particular survey to benchmark with similar colleges and universities regarding programs and services. Residence life is one area in particular where such a tool may be used. The information gathered from a particular national survey instrument provides insights into the satisfaction of students with programs and services offered (e.g., cleanliness of residence halls and quality of food service), but it provides limited information regarding actual learning that may occur as a result of students' interactions with the Department of Residence Life. As a result, this method is not effective for gathering information regarding student learning in a particular residence life program, as the survey (i.e., method) is not tied to the outcomes of any particular program.

Similar to the dichotomy between institutional assessment and programmatic assessment, benchmarking is a useful tool for acquiring information about programs and services; however, the type and scope of the information provided serves a completely different purpose. Outcomes-based assessment leads to gathering evidence to inform specific decisions that will lead to improving specific programs that will heighten student success. Benchmarking employs methods that provide opportunities to compare data across institutions; such data may not readily lead to decisions to improve student success.

The analytical method is most often determined by the nature of the outcome(s) at hand and the comfort of the researcher with the particular method of choice. For example, if institutional leaders are interested in the amount of institutional change in aspects related to student learning and development over time, quantitative methods may be used. Already constructed national survey instruments such as the NSSE, the Cooperative Institutional Research Program Freshmen Survey (CIRP), Your First College Year Survey (YFCY), and the CSS provide valid and reliable tools for assessing related aspects of student learning and development. Outcomes that focus on the nature and detail of a student's learning experiences at colleges and universities may lend themselves more toward qualitative methods. In any case, the type and nature of the data available for use will have a significant impact on the analytical method chosen (Creswell, 1998; Denzin & Lincoln, 2000; Patton, 2002; Pike, 2002).

While it is not the intention of this book to provide an in-depth explanation of the various facets of quantitative and qualitative research design and how they may apply to outcomes-based assessment, a brief overview of each is provided in the sections that follow. These overviews provide a starting point for the reader seeking information about the data collection and analysis process. More complete explanations of quantitative and qualitative tools, data collection, and analysis may be found in the assessment and research methods literature available today (e.g., Creswell, 1998, 2004; Denzin & Lincoln, 2000; Fowler, 1993; Patton, 2002; Stage & Manning, 2003).

Quantitative Assessment Methods

Quantitative methods use numbers for interpreting data (Maki, 2004) and "are distinguished by emphasis on numbers, measurement, experimental design, and statistical analysis" (Palomba & Banta, 1999). Large numbers of cases may be analyzed using quantitative design, and this type of design is deductive in nature, often stemming from a preconceived hypothesis (Patton, 2002). The potential to generalize results to a broader audience and situations makes this type of research/assessment design popular with many. Although assessment can be carried out with the rigor of traditional research, including a hypothesis and results that are statistically significant, this is not a necessary component of programmatic outcomes-based assessment. It is not essential to have a certain sample size unless the scope of your assessment is on the institutional level.

A traditionally favored type of research design that has influenced outcomes-based assessment methodology is quantitative assessment. Quantitative assessment offers a myriad of data collection tools including structured interviews, questionnaires, and tests. In the higher education setting, this type of design is found in many nationally employed assessment tools (e.g., National Survey of Student Engagement, Community College Survey of Student Engagement, and the CORE Institute Alcohol and Drug Survey) but can also be locally developed and used to assess more specific campus needs and student learning outcomes. It is important when engaging in quantitative methodological design, sampling, analysis, and interpretation to ensure that those individuals involved are knowledgeable about, as well as comfortable with, engaging in quantitative design (Palomba & Banta, 1999).

At Colorado State University, two primary quantitative assessment methods are used to examine apartment life on campus. "The Apartment

Life Exit Survey is given to residents as they begin the 'vacate' process from their apartment. Results are tabulated twice each year, once at the end of fall semester and once in the summer" (Bresciani et al., in press).

Administrators at Pennsylvania State University originally measured the success of their newspaper readership program based on satisfaction and use. The quantitative survey they were using was later revised "to include more detailed information on students' readership behavior (e.g., how frequently they are reading a paper, how long, and which sections), students' engagement on campus and in the community, and their self-reported gains in various outcomes (e.g., developing an understanding of current issues, expanding their vocabulary, articulating their views on issues, increasing their reading comprehension)" (Bresciani et al., 2009). This revision allowed them to use survey methodology while still measuring the impact of the program on student learning.

CSUS underwent a similar revision process of a locally developed quantitative survey looking at its new student orientation program. Originally, only student and parent satisfaction were measured. This was later revised to include a true/false component in the orientation evaluation that used a form of indirect assessment. In the final revision, a pre- and posttest were administered to those students attending orientation to measure the knowledge gained in the orientation session (Bresciani et al., 2009).

In addition, a great deal of data already contained in student transactional systems can be used to assist in the evaluation of programs. Data such as facility usage, service usage, adviser notations, participation in student organizations, leadership roles held, and length of community service can all help in explaining why outcomes may have been met. For instance, staff at an institution's counseling service desire for all students who are treated for sexually transmitted diseases to be able to identify the steps and strategies to avoid contracting them before leaving the 45-minute office appointment. However, when they evaluated this, they learned that only 70% of the students were able to do this, but they also examined their office appointment log and realized that because of the high volume of patients, they were only able to spend 27 minutes with each student on average. The decreased intended time to teach students about their well-being may explain why the counseling staff's results were lower than they would have desired.

Qualitative Assessment Methods

According to Denzin and Lincoln (2004), qualitative research is "multi-method in focus, involving an interpretive, naturalistic approach to its subject matter" (p. 2). Upcraft and Schuh (1996) expand this definition by stating, "Qualitative methodology is the detailed description of situations, events, people, interactions, and observed behaviors, the use of direct quotations from people about their experiences, attitudes, beliefs, and thoughts" (p. 21). Qualitative assessment is focused on understanding how people make meaning of and experience their environment or world (Patton, 2002). It is narrow in scope, applicable to specific situations and experiences, and is not intended for generalization to broad situations. Different from quantitative research, qualitative research employs the researcher as the primary means of data collection (e.g., interviews, focus groups, and observations). Also unlike quantitative research, the qualitative approach is inductive in nature, leading to the development or creation of a theory rather than the testing of a preconceived theory or hypothesis (Patton). It is important to note then that when applying qualitative methodology to outcomes-based assessment, you are not fully using an inductive approach because you are using the methodology to determine whether an intended outcome has been identified. However, the application of the methods themselves can yield very rich findings for outcomes-based assessment.

Data for qualitative analysis generally result from fieldwork. According to Patton (2002), during fieldwork a researcher spends a significant amount of time in the setting that is being investigated or examined. Generally multi-method in focus, three types of findings often result from the qualitative fieldwork experience: interviews, observations, and documents.

Each primary type of qualitative data contributes unique and valuable perspectives about student learning to the outcomes-based assessment process. When used in combination, a more complete or holistic picture of student learning is created.

Interviews

Interviews comprise a number of open-ended questions that result in responses that yield information "about people's experiences, perceptions, opinions, feelings, and knowledge" (Patton, 2002, p. 4). It is common to engage in face-to-face verbal interviews with one individual; however, interviews may also be conducted with a group and administered via mail, telephone, or the Web (Upcraft & Schuh, 1996). Though questions and format may differ, an essential component of any interview is the "trust and rapport to be built with respondents" (Upcraft & Schuh, p. 32). Open-ended questions can also be given to students at the conclusion of a program or an event to receive quick and immediate feedback. At Widener University, "questions presented before, during, and after the [student health services] presentations allowed for an interactive experience and a means to monitor learning progress" (Bresciani et al., in press).

Observations

Observations, on the other hand, do not require direct contact with a study participant or group. Rather, this type of data collection involves a researcher providing information-rich descriptions of behavior, conversations, interactions, organizational processes, or any other type of human experience obtained through observation. Such observation may be either *participant*, in which the researcher is actually involved in the activities, conversations, or organizational processes, or *nonparticipant*, in which the research remains on the outside of the activity, conversation, or organizational process in scope (Creswell, 1998; Denzin & Lincoln, 2000; Patton, 2002). In keeping a record of observations, many methods can be used. One way is to take notes during the observation; another method commonly employed is to create a checklist or rubric to use during the observation. The checklist or rubric not only gives the observer a set of criteria to observe, but it also allows the observer to show student progress over time and to correlate a number with a qualitative process. At North Carolina State University, for example,

> a total of 259 students that were found guilty of a violation of the [Student] Code [of Conduct] were assigned a paper with questions specifically written to correspond with the criteria for the development of insight and impact on life issues, as identified in the learning outcome. A rubric was used to review the papers. The rubric was created based on a theory of insight by Mary M. Murray (1995). In her book *Artwork of the Mind*, Murray describes how to determine the development of insight through writing. Initially 20 papers were drawn randomly to test the rubric. The rubric originally had a scale with three categories: beginning, developing and achieved and six dimensions based on the theory and practice. In total, 22 papers were drawn and reviewed based on the rubric. (Bresciani et al., 2009)

Isothermal Community College (ICC) incorporated the qualitative assessment method of using portfolios for professionals completing the assessment process. Although this particular example focuses on staff and departments using portfolios, this method of assessment is commonly used with students as well. At ICC

> each year staff set aside time to reflect on what has been learned through assessment, compile related documents into a portfolio, and summarize major areas of learning into what we refer to as "reflective narratives." The process is systematic and ongoing with portfolios and narratives submitted for review by various administrators in June of each year. (Bresciani et al., 2009)

Documents

Finally, documents include "written materials and other documents from organizational, clinical, or programs records; memoranda and correspondence; official publications and reports; personal diaries, letters, artistic works, photographs, and memorabilia; and written responses to open-ended surveys" (Patton, 2002, p. 4). Public records and personal documents are the two primary categories of documents one might use when doing outcomes-based assessment or research (Upcraft & Schuh, 1996). Newspaper and magazine excerpts, enrollment and retention records, and campus safety reports are examples of public records commonly found on college and university campuses. Student health records, grades, and judicial records are examples of personal records. Both types of documents can enhance the overall data collected in an assessment project. It is important to note, however, that the authenticity of documents must be determined prior to using them for assessment (Creswell, 1998; Patton, 2002; Upcraft & Schuh, 1996).

In addition to the aforementioned documents, many student affairs professionals also use portfolios, student reflections, reports, or other forms of classroom-type documents for outcomes-based assessment data collection. Again, criteria checklists or rubrics can be used in the analysis of documents to identify whether outcomes are met. Keep in mind that whenever criteria are used with a qualitative method, the process of inductive discovery is diminished and therefore so is the true nature of the qualitative methodology. Nonetheless, documents are a rich source of information and provide a great starting point for any assessment project.

Criteria to Consider When Choosing and Employing Methods

Simply choosing a method or methods to use when engaging in outcomes-based assessment is not enough to ensure the method chosen will effectively serve its intended purpose. Therefore, it is necessary to examine the following guidelines to inform your efforts when choosing and employing methods for outcomes-based assessment in student affairs. Regardless of the type of research methods chosen, a number of considerations must be taken into account when choosing appropriate research methods. First, it is important to consider whether to use direct or indirect methods or a combination of both to assess student learning. Direct methods (e.g., naturally occurring methods) necessitate that students demonstrate knowledge and skills acquired through a particular experience as they respond to a particular instrument. These are methods that "include both *objective tests* where students select a response from among those provided and *performance measures* where students generate their own responses" (Palomba & Banta, 1999, p. 12). Examples of performance measures include multiple-choice exams, electronic portfolios, essay questions, and reflection papers that allow for the demonstration of skills and knowledge. Indirect measures, in turn, are those that require students to reflect on learning as opposed to actually displaying or demonstrating that learning. Exit interviews and alumni surveys are just two of the many types of indirect methods discussed in the literature. The following lists provide the most common methods used for outcomes-based assessment and suggested guidelines for consideration when selecting these methods.

Surveys

- The type of survey (local or commercially developed) is congruent with the purpose of the outcomes-based assessment task at hand.
- The survey is valid or measures what it is intended to measure.
- The survey is reliable or elicits consistent responses to questions about the same topic.
- The survey is affordable and may be administered in a timely manner.
- Fiscal and human resources are available for proper scoring of the survey results (Schuh & Upcraft, 2001).
- You can identify specific questions in the survey that when answered will allow you to identify whether the outcome has been met.

- You can identify specific questions in the survey that when answered will allow you to identify how to improve the program that was intended to meet the outcome.

Interviews

- The questions effectively address the topic at hand.
- The interview has a mix of structured and unstructured questions.
- The interview is not overly cumbersome or too time intensive for the participant.
- The questions are clear and concise and avoid language that is misleading, confusing, or unethical.
- The sequence of the questions is efficient and moves well from one topic to the next (Schuh & Upcraft, 2001).
- You can identify specific questions in the interview protocol that when answered will allow you to identify whether the outcome has been met.
- You can identify specific questions in the interview protocol that when answered will allow you to identify how to improve the program that was intended to meet the outcome.

Focus Groups

- The information sought is about student perceptions, attitudes, beliefs, opinions, and/or experiences.
- The topic at hand is one that participants are comfortable discussing in a public forum.
- The information garnered will provide insight for planning programs or initiatives in student affairs/services.
- The information sought is not statistical in nature.
- Ample time and resources are available for the planning and implementation of the focus group.
- A reasonable number of participants and an informed facilitator will be present.
- An appropriate mixture of structured and unstructured questions is developed.
- Questions are effectively sequenced and ample time is available for discussion (Schuh & Upcraft, 2001).

- You can identify specific questions in the interview protocol that when answered will allow you to identify whether the outcome has been met.
- You can identify specific questions in the interview protocol that when answered will allow you to identify how to improve the program that was intended to meet the outcome.

Observation

- The setting is one in which the identified learning outcomes may be observed.
- The setting is one in which the student affairs/services program or service may potentially have an impact on student learning and development.
- You can apply specific criteria that when identified will allow you to determine whether the outcome has been met.
- You can apply specific criteria that when identified will allow you to determine how to improve the program that was intended to meet the outcome.

Journal Reflections or Portfolio Reflections

- The question/concept participants respond to stems from the learning outcomes articulated in the assessment plan.
- The reflection questions/concept are designed to demonstrate learning as a result of participation in a student affairs program, service, or activity and not as a result of extraneous experiences or activities.
- The reflections are analyzed by unbiased assessment experts well versed in identifying themes and ideas that emerge from the participants' writing.
- You can apply specific criteria that when identified will allow you to determine whether the outcome has been met.
- You can apply specific criteria that when identified will allow you to determine how to improve the program that was intended to meet the outcome.

Role Plays or Case Study Discussions

- The role plays and case study discussions are designed to demonstrate whether students effectively grasped the concepts, ideas, and behaviors specified in the learning outcomes developed for a particular program, service, or activity.

- The role plays and case study discussions are analyzed by unbiased professionals well versed in the intended outcomes and expectations of the program or experience at hand.
- You can apply specific criteria that when identified will allow you to determine whether the outcome has been met.
- You can apply specific criteria that when identified will allow you to determine how to improve the program that was intended to meet the outcome.

Document Analysis/Portfolio Artifacts

- The purpose of the document is congruent with the learning outcomes at hand.
- The document contains information that informs the outcomes-based assessment process.
- The information garnered is relevant to the learning outcomes set forth (Schuh & Upcraft, 2001).
- You can apply specific criteria checklists or rubrics that when identified will allow you to determine whether the outcome has been met.
- You can apply specific criteria checklists or rubrics that when identified will allow you to determine how to improve the program that was intended to meet the outcome.

Triangulation

Regardless of the method(s) chosen, it is always a good idea to gather information about student learning using several methods and from multiple sources (Maki, 2004). This results in a much more complete picture of overall student learning and development than the information provided by only one method. Triangulation is a process by which you substantiate the findings of one assessment method with one or more other sources or assessment methods (Creswell, 2004). If institution administrators decided to use a mixed-methods approach, incorporating qualitative and quantitative assessment methods, it would essentially be considered triangulation. Triangulation of assessment methods can be conducted simultaneously. For example, at ICC

> there are many methods for assessing learning and student satisfaction outcomes statements related to financial aid. Several of these methods are: (1)

Survey and focus group feedback is reviewed carefully for insight regarding student learning as it relates to financial aid services. (2) The percentage of the ICC student body receiving financial aid is monitored. (3) Benchmarking data is considered: (a) Pell disbursed is compared among institutions of similar size in North Carolina. (b) National trends related to the average amount of financial aid disbursed in public 2-year colleges are considered. (Bresciani et al., 2009)

Triangulation can also be conducted separately. This means that you may initially use only one method of assessment (e.g., survey); however, findings of that assessment method may yield more questions. In this instance, further assessment methods (e.g., pre-/posttest, observation, and focus groups) could be used to corroborate those results. For example, you may administer a quantitative survey regarding the campus climate for women. Once you analyze the results of that survey, the exact factors enhancing or detracting from an overall positive campus environment may still remain unclear. In an effort to learn more specific information about the factors that contribute to or detract from a positive campus experience, you may develop focus group questions that delve further into the issues at hand. This added step of a focus group can provide more specific information and clarification of the survey data. In so doing, it will contribute to the triangulation of the data.

While not considered a practice of triangulation, in outcomes-based assessment you can authenticate findings when various parties use the same methodology and criteria. For example, you may use a rubric to assess the public-speaking skills of students in a university seminar class. The data will be considered authentic if

1. Peers who did not teach your students rate the students on their public-speaking skills.
2. You, the instructor, rate their public-speaking skills.
3. Other students in the class rate each other on public-speaking skills.

Only one method of assessment was used—the rubric. However, data were gathered from three different sources: other instructors, yourself, and students in the class.

When using triangulation or methods to authenticate your findings, keep in mind that the purpose of triangulation and authentication is to verify and demonstrate the trustworthiness of the decisions derived from your assessment data. Therefore, consider using other professionals, students, and even published literature to interpret the results and make decisions. This will allow for quality control. When all else fails, remember that you will check the quality of the decision you made when you reassess the outcome, whether the very next semester, year, or 3 years down the road. Upon reexamination of the outcome, you will be able to determine whether the decision you made actually led to the improvement you intended.

Additional Considerations

When choosing an assessment method, it is important to remember that it is not necessary to re-create the wheel. Many assessment tools already exist in addition to national assessment surveys. By simply conducting a search of resources available online or within your own institution, much time and effort can be saved if such a tool already exists. If you do create your own tools, guides and resources are also available to assist in this process, such as on-campus experts, rubric generators, or tools to help in the creation of surveys. The majority of these resources can be found by conducting an online search (see chapter 11 for online search resources). Keep in mind that when you borrow an already created assessment tool, be sure to cite the creator of the tool. And be sure to adapt the tool to your specific assessment situation. If you find the tool fits your needs exactly without adaptation, then consider comparing data with the institution you borrowed the tool from. Sharing the tool and the exchange of comparative data may lead to even richer decisions for improving student success.

Those engaged in the assessment process should attend to resource and time challenges that may exist. It is important to understand what financial and human resources are available prior to developing any outcomes-based assessment design. Additionally, the time available for the assessment process as a whole should be considered in an effort to ensure that all steps in the process (e.g., instrument creation, implementation, data collection, analysis, and decision making) may be completed in their entirety.

5

UTILIZATION AND DISSEMINATION OF RESULTS

Outcomes-based assessment requires the involvement of many to ensure that assessment efforts do not fall by the wayside once the data collection and interpretation of results are complete. After collecting and interpreting assessment results, one must involve others in determining how the results will be used as well as in effectively communicating the results and decisions to institutional and community stakeholders (Bresciani et al., 2004; Palomba & Banta, 1999; Suskie, 2004; Upcraft & Schuh, 1996). The effective execution of this final step is of paramount importance, as this will contribute to increased acceptance of the assessment process in general, which will affirm organizational commitment to evidence-based decision making to improve student learning and success. Such a practice allows for the effective use of the results to enhance student learning (Bresciani et al.). Palomba and Banta concluded that "widespread engagement helps guarantee that assessment will focus on the most important learning issues and maximizes the likelihood that assessment information will be used" (p. 10). Additionally, such engagement will ensure that the results are disseminated effectively and that future assessment builds upon current results where appropriate.

Identifying the Stakeholders

A number of parties should be included in the use and dissemination of the results. Bennion and Harris (2005) state that creating a culture of assessment often results in many challenges (discussed in chapter 8). According to the authors, such challenges may be addressed by taking a comprehensive approach toward the assessment process that encourages faculty, staff, and administrative ownership. The authors of this book take the insights of Bennion and Harris (2005) one step further and include students, parents, and other institutional constituents, such as community partners, employers, and those who choose to invest in student learning, in the group of primary stakeholders, who should be involved in the outcomes-based assessment process. Each of these parties is reviewed in greater detail in the paragraphs that follow.

Though many stakeholders are identified, each stakeholder may not be involved in every aspect of the outcomes-based assessment process. Rather, the context and goals of each assessment project should be considered to determine which stakeholders should be involved at each step. It is key to remember that any individual or group affected by the assessment results should be involved in the process (Jacobi, Astin, & Ayala, 1987). Maki (2004) states, "Expanding the range of contributors brings different lenses to assessing student learning that broaden interpretations of student achievement" (p. 7). Therefore, it is advisable to include those stakeholders who will provide the best overall picture of student learning and development on each campus. In this section we highlight the myriad of stakeholders who may be involved in the process and provide a discussion of their unique contributions to the outcomes-based assessment process. Prior to beginning that discussion, however, we suggest considering the following questions when selecting stakeholders for each step of the outcomes-based assessment process:

1. What individuals, groups, offices, or departments might be affected by the outcomes-based assessment process?
2. How might representatives from such groups contribute to the outcomes-based assessment process?
3. What other stakeholders can we partner with to develop and implement an effective outcomes-based assessment process?
4. What resources are available to promote and secure acceptance and involvement by stakeholders?
5. What resources and insights might our stakeholders provide for the outcomes-based assessment process?

6. What is the best use of stakeholder time and talent during the outcomes-based assessment process, and how can we maximize the use of each?

Student Affairs Administrators

This book supports the notion that outcomes-based assessment of learning in student affairs is necessary to truly understand the ways cocurricular programs and services contribute to the overall learning and development of students in postsecondary learning environments. Therefore, it is prudent that those responsible for designing the cocurriculum—student affairs administrators—be involved in the creation and implementation of assessment efforts as well as the dissemination and implementation of results. Officials at North Carolina State University reiterate this when they say that "everyone should be involved with assessment, including senior student affairs administrators. If the process is not important to whom the units report, then it is extremely difficult to convince the units that assessment should be a priority" (Bresciani et al., 2009). Maki (2004) states that campus leaders, such as vice presidents, deans, and department heads, are responsible for establishing systems of communication, campus agendas, and campus priorities. Consequently, the chief student affairs officer must lead any assessment efforts to ensure the results are effectively disseminated and used for enhancement of student learning.

Department heads should also take an active role in ensuring that members of their departments are aware of the assessment results. Frequent communication about assessment processes and results, coupled with discussion about continuous improvement efforts informed by assessment results, will keep assessment efforts at the forefront. Moore Gardner (2006) highlighted the idea of *nucleators*, or small groups of people who exemplify or embrace an idea throughout an institutional hierarchy. Identification of a few key nucleators within a department or division who are interested in and willing to assist with dissemination and use efforts will strengthen ownership in the assessment of the student learning process, thereby ingraining assessment efforts deeper into the fabric of an institution and creating a culture of continuous improvement.

For example, creating a divisional assessment team (e.g., Student Affairs Assessment Team) composed of one or two individuals from each department who are interested in and support outcomes-based assessment can really help in the promotion and implementation of assessment plans as well as with data collection, analysis, and information dissemination. Not only can this group assist the individual or individuals in charge of the overall assessment process, these nucleators can work with peers they respect and may regularly work with to make the assessment process meaningful and to promote peers' acceptance of it. By learning about the merits of outcomes-based assessment through peers, those who may otherwise balk at the prospect of adding another task to their already full plates or who may be less likely to accept new tasks from a senior-level administrator they may not have direct contact with may more readily embrace the assessment process.

Faculty

Faculty members are a second group of stakeholders whose participation in the use and dissemination process is important. In her book titled *Outcomes-Based Academic and Co-curricular Program Review*, Bresciani (2006) noted that 100% of the good-practice institutions indicated that it is "somewhat important" to "very important" for cocurricular and academic departments to collaborate in the assessment process. Student learning does not just take place inside or outside the classroom. Rather, learning is transcendent, crossing in- and out-of-classroom boundaries to create a holistic growth and development process. It is, therefore, important for student affairs administrators to partner with faculty colleagues when disseminating and using information about student learning.

Staff at Northern Arizona University acknowledged that "faculty are more invested when they are involved in assessment from the beginning" (Bresciani et al., 2009). At Paradise Valley Community College,

> several student affairs programs have faculty as members of advisory committees and there is faculty representation on the out of class assessment committee. Faculty have played key roles in evaluating the effectiveness of such programs as intercollegiate athletics, service learning, the child development center, and academic advising. Faculty review and provide feedback on the out of class assessment plans and reports. (Bresciani et al.)

Still other institutions reported having faculty involved in planning orientation as representatives on the judicial board, on advising committees, and in living-learning communities. Officials at Texas A&M recognized that "the difference between cooperation, collaboration and integration was not clearly defined when it [came] to reporting faculty involvement in the Division of Student Affairs. Many [used] the terms interchangeably when in reality they [reflected] very different relationships" (Bresciani et al.).

Haessig and La Potin (2004) acknowledged that faculty involvement in assessment of student learning is critical to success but often difficult to attain. They suggest a number of methods for securing faculty engagement, including understanding and addressing faculty concerns and educating faculty about the purpose of assessment efforts in student affairs. Conveying a sense of urgency and encouraging faculty ownership through the entire assessment process are additional methods for increasing faculty involvement. Finally, obtaining overall institutional support for outcomes-based assessment in student affairs will demonstrate that it is an institutional priority, which may in turn encourage more faculty members to get involved (Haessig & La Potin). Faculty members are often well versed in research and assessment methods and may have many ideas for effective dissemination of results. Encouraging ownership by tapping into their thoughts and ideas about assessment of student learning contributes to an effective assessment process. It may also create and strengthen important institutional partnerships. For more information on collaborative approaches to assessment, see chapter 9.

Students

Students are important stakeholders in the dissemination and use of assessment results; however, they are often overlooked. According to Maki (2004) "a collective institutional commitment to assessing student learning engages all who contribute to the educational process, including students themselves" (p. 7). As those enmeshed in the assessment process, we often ask students for their insights about learning and development but fail to share the results of those efforts with the students. Students, however, view the assessment results through yet another lens and could provide novel suggestions for means of effectively using the results.

Palomba and Banta (1999) concur, stating that students should be involved in decision making surrounding the assessment processes. Students may be more apt to provide meaningful input if they understand the assessment process, how the information will be used, and why such processes are important to their learning and development. Involving students in the assessment process builds important partnerships and allows students to actively engage in the creation and enhancement of their cocurricular experiences (Bresciani et al., 2009; Palomba & Banta, 2004; Upcraft & Schuh, 1996).

Students may get involved in the process in a number of ways. At Frederick Community College, "many assessment measures utilized involve student rating of criteria identified to measure the expected outcomes" (Bresciani et al., in press). Inviting student representatives to sit on departmental, divisional, and university assessment committees is another common and easy way to get students involved. Other suggestions include asking members of student government or other student organizations to identify what they believe students learn as a result of participating in particular activities and experiences. Students' insight about what they believe they are getting out of their collegiate endeavors may differ from that of student affairs professionals and faculty and may contribute to the creation of additional learning outcomes that might otherwise be overlooked. Administrators at Oregon State University found this quite successful, where some departments have

> asked students what they wanted to learn from particular experiences, employment, or leadership positions and then worked with the students to design experiences to deliver those outcomes. Some have made it a point to provide the results of their assessments to students, while others have used assessment results as talking points when engaging with students about services or programs. (Bresciani et al.)

Getting students in a classroom setting involved by partnering with a faculty member to have students in a particular course provide thoughts about learning outcomes or novel assessment methods provides the twofold benefit of collaborating among divisions as well as highlighting new ideas for learning outcomes and methods of measurement.

Finally, partnering with students in the dissemination of results is another way to get students engaged in the process. Working with student government and programming boards to enhance programming or experiences based on the results of assessment in student affairs is a unique way to promote student involvement (Bresciani et al., 2004). It is important when involving students to do more than use the traditional means of involvement such as inviting students to sit on committees and boards. Getting student government and other groups involved is just one way that students may be integrated into the assessment process.

Other Stakeholders

According to Bender, Lowery, and Schuh (2005), a number of direct and indirect groups are stakeholders in higher education. Therefore, it is important to also consider those groups that may be indirectly involved in and affected by higher education. Such stakeholders include parents and relatives of students, state legislators, state and government agencies, and members of the community. Each of these groups provides unique perspectives and may have dissimilar expectations and goals for student learning, such as employers and graduate schools (Bender et al.).

In addition to student affairs administrators, faculty members, and students, members of the board of trustees should be involved in the assessment process. Though not always involved in the beginning stages of the process, these parties need to be informed about the findings and use of outcomes-based assessment results. According to Maki (2004), it is the responsibility of boards of trustees to learn about student achievement and to be champions of institutional quality. The results of outcomes-based assessment in student affairs help identify the ways the cocurricular environment enhances and encourages student learning. Boards of trustees can use such information when making fiscal decisions and demonstrating accountability to state and federal governments. Outcomes-based assessment results may also be used to set institutional priorities and to allocate or reallocate resources (Maki).

Another important group of stakeholders in the outcomes-based assessment process is senior leaders such as presidents, vice presidents, provosts, and deans. These individuals determine organizational structure, set institutional priorities and policies, create channels of communication, and oversee the business of the university or college in general (Maki, 2004). Much of the initiative, support, and resources for outcomes-based assessment, then, stems from members of this group. Therefore, it is imperative that key senior leaders are involved in and support the assessment process from the beginning. Though these individuals will, most likely, not be the people directing and carrying out the assessment process, senior leaders should be consulted regularly and kept abreast of overall progress made, findings, challenges, and use of the findings. Such information will help inform future initiatives, budgeting, programs, and services that have an impact on student learning.

Additionally, as mentioned previously, senior leaders' support (verbal and resourcewise) of outcomes-based assessment is necessary for the livelihood of any assessment process. For these reasons, keeping an open line of communication with senior leaders throughout the assessment cycle or process is recommended.

Parents and family members of students may be involved in the assessment process or, at a minimum, have their perspectives considered during the process. In recent years, there has been a notable increase in parent and family involvement in the college experience. Bender and Schuh (2005) assert that though their interests in particular campus issues vary extensively, "the parents of college students have become a vocal constituency that higher education leaders cannot afford to ignore" (p. 214). It is necessary, therefore, to listen to this constituent group to learn about its expectations for higher education in general and student learning more specifically. Parent focus groups, informal and formal conversations during new student orientation, and phone or e-mail solicitations for input about outcomes are just a few of the ways this increasingly vocal group can be involved in the outcomes-based assessment process.

Finally, depending upon the assessment task at hand, other stakeholders besides student affairs administrators, faculty, and students may be involved. Institutional alumni, student employers, and community members may also be included in the information dissemination and results implementation processes (Palomba & Banta, 1999). External accrediting agencies and state and federal governments are other stakeholders that may at times be included in the information-sharing process. Though not involved in every assessment process, some projects may affect the work of stakeholders. In such cases, it is necessary to keep relevant parties abreast of information that may be used to enhance their work with students.

Additional Tips for Getting Stakeholders Involved

Palomba and Banta (1999) assert, "Of all the important factors in creating a successful assessment program, none matters more than widespread involvement of those who are affected by it" (p. 53). A challenge, however, often lies in actually getting important stakeholders involved in the process. Busy schedules, limited understanding of the merit of assessment, and an already overtaxed group of stakeholders make getting those who truly need to be engaged in the process extremely difficult at times (Palomba & Banta, 1999; Schuh & Upcraft, 2001). The following sections offer additional suggestions to assist in the acquisition of necessary stakeholders in the assessment process.

Educate

Student affairs professionals can be a difficult group of stakeholders to engage in the assessment process. These are the individuals most likely to see the fruit of their labor not only in the communication of the results but also in the use of the results for evaluation and change purposes. Despite understanding the merit of assessment, these professionals already have an overwhelming amount of responsibility and may be resistant to adding yet another responsibility (Schuh & Upcraft, 2001). Faculty, likewise, are inundated with the pressures of teaching, research, and service and may hesitate when invited to participate in the process. Students, in turn, may not see the need to be involved in the assessment process or may not even realize they are actually active participants whose insights and suggestions can greatly enhance any outcomes-based assessment project.

For these and other tentative stakeholders, you may increase their willingness to get involved by demonstrating the ways assessment efforts can be used to inform everyday professional activities such as budgeting, strategic planning, and programming. For those individuals who may continue to drag their feet, educating them about the overall merit of assessment (e.g., demonstrating cocurricular contributions to learning, increasing partnerships among faculty and administrators, and enhancing the student experience) and the many benefits it provides might be helpful. Finding peers (e.g., other administrators, willing faculty, and students interested in leadership experiences) who are eager to be engaged and who may be able to connect with those who are not so enthusiastic and find a way to reach them is also a means of getting more people on board. Educating others about assessment and fostering acceptance of it is of paramount importance in this process. The more people know about the assessment process, the less likely they are to have excuses not to do it (Palomba & Banta, 1999). By reiterating that assessment is a means for student affairs professionals and faculty to demonstrate what they are already doing—contributing to student learning and development—and that outcomes-based assessment is simply a way to share these contributions with others, it may be easier to achieve involvement in the assessment process.

Communicate

In addition to educating, communicating a clear commitment to assessment from the senior-level leadership throughout the entire institution is important. A statement by a college dean giving advice for getting faculty involved may be applied to all stakeholders: "You have to let faculty know that assessment is a serious endeavor, and you have to be willing to repeat yourself" (Palomba & Banta, 1999, p. 67). Convincing stakeholders that assessment is not a trend but a process with the intention of enmeshment in the fabric of the organization will increase involvement levels. Wasting time on the latest idea or fleeting notion is not looked upon kindly by administrators, faculty, students, or other stakeholders in the assessment process. Therefore, it is necessary and important to secure participation by clearly articulating and demonstrating the long-term commitment to assessment as a tool for institutional enhancement.

More importantly, communicating the results of assessment and how such results are used for improvement and/or change will also demonstrate to stakeholders the utility of the process. Additionally, it will reinforce to those who participate in the assessment process, such as faculty and administrators, that their efforts and commitments are worthwhile. They actually see the results of their efforts being used to inform decisions, recommendations, and resource reallocations. Through this they clearly see that they are no longer just filing reports but contributing to action and the formation of a student-learning-centered culture.

Communication of results is also a key strategy for getting students on board with the assessment process. It is often the case that we put assessment measures in place without considering the impact it has on the already overtested and overanalyzed student body. By articulating the goals of assessment at the beginning and following up with a review of how the results are used to improve students' collegiate experiences, they may develop an understanding of and appreciation for the myriad of ways their contributions to the process yield benefits for the campus as a whole (Bresciani et al., 2004; Maki, 2004). Involving students in formulating the actual decisions that are made based on outcomes assessment provides even more enthusiasm for and acceptance of assessment.

Ways to Disseminate Results of Assessment

Palomba and Banta (1999) argue that the "assessment information is of little use if it is not shared with appropriate audiences and used in meaningful ways" (p. 297). Assessment results may be disseminated in a variety of ways contingent upon the assessment project at hand, the stakeholders involved, and the political realities that may exist in a given institution, division, or department. It is important to triangulate information-sharing efforts to ensure that the most information is shared with the largest number of constituents. Whatever the means for communicating results, one must consider the audience and the type of information to be shared in order to provide information that is clear and understandable.

Moreover, it is necessary that a number of different parties in an institution (e.g., administrators, faculty, and students) undertake the interpretation of data. This will help ensure that all possible conclusions regarding the data are drawn (Palomba & Banta, 1999). For example, sharing the results with a number of constituents (e.g., a faculty member, an administrator not involved in the assessment process, a student, and an alumnus or alumna) and asking them to read the results and provide their conclusions without seeing those of others may yield unexpected insights and suggestions on how to use the findings for evaluation purposes.

Departmental, divisional, and university-wide newsletters are a common means for communicating assessment results (Bennion & Harris, 2003). Such newsletters may range in frequency from monthly to bimonthly to once per semester or academic year. Face-to-face presentations or meetings are another means of sharing assessment results. Green, Jones, and Pascarell (2005) advocate assessment workshops, which contribute to acceptance for the assessment process in general, and they provide open forums for results to be shared and discussed, plans for the effective use of results, and any ambiguities or concerns to be aired. Similar to newsletters, meetings and presentations may vary in size and scope depending on the audience and the information at hand. Campuswide e-mails are an additional avenue for information sharing. This is a quick and inexpensive way to share information with small groups or the entire university. Incorporating celebrated results on the institution's Web site will also allow students, student affairs professionals, community members, faculty, and other stakeholders to see the focus on and contributions to student learning and development at your institution.

Again, no matter how one chooses to share the information, it is important to take into consideration the makeup of the various audiences the assessment results will be shared with and to communicate the results in a way all parties can understand. This will dictate the methods used for communicating results with stakeholders.

Use of Results

Just as institutional context and culture must be considered when deciding how to communicate assessment results with stakeholders, they are equally important when formulating ways to effectively use results. Though it would seem only practical that institutions use the results of their outcomes-based assessments to enhance and improve student learning experiences, it is not uncommon for assessment to stall at this phase (Upcraft & Schuh, 1996). The failure to make the transition from gathering results to using those results to make informed decisions may cause apathy on the part of stakeholders who are disenfranchised because little to no change occurs as a result of simply gathering information.

For example, in a scenario familiar to many, institutions may administer a number of surveys each year to students; however, once the results of those surveys are calculated, they are reviewed by the vice president and a few administrators in a division and then put on a shelf or locked in a filing cabinet. No dissemination of results to stakeholders occurs, and no visible change resulting from those findings is initiated. This may contribute to reduced acceptance of assessment in student affairs and create dissonance regarding squandered resources and time. It is therefore beneficial not only for enhancing student learning experiences but also for maintaining or increasing support for outcomes-based assessment in general that the results be used effectively.

A number of key factors contribute to the effective use of assessment results. An organized and specific assessment report that includes the use of assessment results should be outlined in the beginning. Such a report with questions for consideration should include, at a basic level, the following components:

1. Program name with a key person's name and contact information
2. Departmental or program mission
   a. How does this mission fit in with the division or institutional mission?
3. Departmental or program goals
   a. How are our goals linked to institutional/divisional goals and/or strategic initiatives?
4. Learning outcomes
   a. How are the learning outcomes linked to the department or program goals?
5. Methods for collecting data
   a. Who collected the data and when were they collected?
   b. What methods were employed (e.g., survey, focus group, or interviews)?
   c. How were the data analyzed and when were they analyzed?
   d. How were the data authenticated?
   e. Who analyzed the data?
   f. What were the limitations of data collection and analysis, if any?
6. Results
   a. What were the results as they relate to the outcomes being measured?
   b. What else was learned from this process that may inform the outcomes?
   c. What other types of data can be gathered from the institutional databases that may help inform decisions around this outcome?
   d. What institutional performance indicators can the results of this assessment report inform?
   e. With whom will the results be shared?
   f. Who needs to be given a heads-up about forthcoming results? Or who needs a preview of the results?
   g. How do the results inform institutional/divisional goals or strategic initiatives? Who needs to know about that connection?
   h. What is the timeline for sharing results with each group?
   i. How will the results be shared?
7. Recommendations and decisions
   a. What changes, if any, should be made to the program? Who will make those changes? How much will those changes cost? Where will the resources come from?

b. What recommendations need to be made if the locus of control for improvement resides outside of our department? To whom should those recommendations be made? In what context should they be made and when?

c. If the results did help measure institutional/divisional goals or strategic priorities, who needs to be involved in the decisions made as a result of that connection?

d. What changes, if any, should be made to the assessment plan?

e. What was effective or ineffective, efficient or inefficient?

f. What comments/discussion points from decision makers need to be recorded so that we can be mindful of what the next steps should be?

8. Implementation of revised plan

a. Who is responsible for implementing the decisions and recommendations for enhancing student learning and development?

b. What priority for implementation does this plan have?

c. How does implementation fit into the institutional/divisional goals and strategic priorities?

d. When will it be done?

This outline and questions may help guide those involved in assessment during the entire process and will lessen the possibility of leaving out a step or not completing the task at hand.

The commitment of institutional leadership to hearing and responding to the recommendations drawn from an assessment project is important (Upcraft & Schuh, 1996). As echoed throughout this book, the lack of top-down commitment to assessment is likely to stagnate progress and almost ensures failure of the assessment process. Additionally, input by key stakeholders throughout the entire process and, most specifically, the conclusion-drawing, results, and use stages will ensure that all potential avenues for use are discussed and taken.

Accountability for what is done and not done in regard to results use will also encourage those spearheading the assessment process to use the results in a meaningful manner. Palomba and Banta (1999) suggested considering the context and culture of an individual campus when determining what types of actions will encourage the use of assessment results. For example, linking the use of results to the strategic planning or continuous improvement processes may help members of the campus community understand the significance of assessment to institutional growth and development. Additionally, tying assessment results to budgeting and funding sends a clear message about the importance of assessment and the use of the results to the daily activity of student affairs and to institutions of higher education in general (Palomba & Banta). Finally, establishing deadlines for the process as a whole will ensure that data collection, interpretation, and use happen in a timely manner, and that the results will be used when they are most relevant to the institution and its constituents (Upcraft & Schuh, 1996).

The following is a summary of the steps recommended for the use process:

1. Compile a complete list or a report of *all* outcomes-based assessment results.
2. Consider the resources (human, financial, time) available for using results for change.
3. Include the necessary stakeholders throughout the use process. This includes determining how the results will be used as well as ensuring follow-through for the entire process.
4. Establish deadlines for the use process and evaluate the effectiveness of the process as well as any changes made according to that deadline.
5. Use the results in a manner that produces the greatest change and enhancements in student learning and development.

Potential Pitfalls of Results Use and Dissemination

Minor tasks can turn into major headaches if not tended to effectively and, therefore, must be considered when using and disseminating results. How results will be presented and shared and with whom must be carefully determined. Any higher education environment is a political enclave and one must carefully consider the ramifications of sharing the results, good or bad, in terms of timing, method, and audience. For example, if an assessment cycle concludes with results that are not favorable for one particular program or service, it is important to share those results with the director or head of that program or department prior to sharing the information publicly with the institution as a whole. It may also be a good idea to work with that director to put steps in place to respond to the issue at hand so that stakeholders, once aware of the issue of concern, will also know that the issue will be addressed appropriately.

In terms of timing, the senior-level leadership should always be the first, outside those actually involved in the assessment process, to see the results. This will keep them abreast of any findings, good and bad, they may want to address with institutional stakeholders, including trustees or members of the community. It will also provide useful information that can be used to inform the planning and budgeting process throughout the year. Failing to keep senior leaders in the loop may result in the misallocation of resources to programs and services that do not enhance learning as intended or believed to. In addition to senior leaders, it is necessary to consider the other stakeholders who should be informed of assessment results and when such stakeholders should hear of them. Some form of public sharing of assessment results should take place each year to keep the institutional communities informed. Newsletters, public forums, and discussion of results at student organization, departmental, and other meetings are a few means of communicating results.

Additionally, the results do not change for each audience you present the information to. However, you may present the information in different ways depending on the makeup of the audience. When presenting to senior-level administrators, for example, it is important to present the information in a professional and easy-to-follow format. We suggest beginning with a simple and concise format of three bullet points of results followed by three bullet points of suggested actions. This should be followed by an executive summary of the outcomes-based assessment process and results, as well as a complete report of the findings, suggestions for use, and the stakeholders the results should be disseminated to. This differs from a presentation to members of the board of trustees in which you might use a summary of statistics and graphs or charts to show the overall impact on student learning. You might also use student quotes when highlighting the same information for a student audience in the school newspaper.

In addition, transparency and stakeholder acceptance are also important. It is important to identify particular stakeholder values and to align the need for the action(s) recommended with the values of the stakeholders. This will enhance acceptance and increase the potential for change that results from the outcomes-based assessment process. The transparency of the results is often a valued ideal in an institution's culture. Therefore, the reader should pay careful attention to involving the stakeholders at just the right time in an effort to encourage transparency while also ensuring that the information is shared appropriately and in the most meaningful manner with all members of the university or college community.

A last suggestion that seems trivial but is very important is to label all assessment document items with "Draft" until finalized recommendations are made. This will ensure that the information provided to those outside an assessment committee or to a director is understood to be in progress and that conclusions are not set in stone until they are reviewed and reflected upon by all of the necessary parties. It will also help guard against misinterpretation of information, which can often happen in any assessment or review process.

Linking the Results to Planning Priorities and the Allocation of Resources

As noted frequently throughout this chapter, the use and dissemination of results is a very important step in the outcomes-based assessment cycle. If done well, this phase can set the stage for important improvements, in addition to validating the importance of assessment in demonstrating the significant ways student affairs work contributes to student learning and development. If done poorly or not at all, the entire assessment process can be undermined, resources can be wasted, and positive and constructive messages may not be shared with those who need to hear them. Therefore, it is imperative to ensure that this step in the process is completed effectively and that all important stakeholders are involved during the appropriate time.

Yet, given all the advice in this chapter, if the results generated from outcomes-based assessment are not linked to decisions that reinforce divisional strategic initiatives and planning priorities, the process loses its ability to truly change an organization's focus on improving student success. In other words, if the advice outlined in chapters 3 and 6 is not heeded, an organization may end up with several recommendations or decisions for improvement and no way to link them to its mission, planning priorities, or strategic objectives. Then, leadership simply becomes overwhelmed by the good ideas the results of outcomes-based assessment generate and is not able to focus the reallocation of its resources to its priorities for improvement.

After hearing the plenary presentation that led to the article "Presenting General Learning Within a Bottom-Line Business World" (Bresciani, 2008-b, 2008-c), a colleague approached the podium and announced, "Industry graveyards are littered with projects that resulted from good ideas; some of them data driven in their design. So, why do we think that in higher education, every good idea we generate should be implemented?" The paraphrased version of this colleague's statement reinforces the emphasis that we need to place on prioritizing the decisions and recommendations resulting from outcomes-based assessment in accordance with the priorities of the division or institution.

Indeed, many great ideas on how to improve student success will be derived from systematic outcomes-based assessment. And many of them will not be able to be implemented because of a lack of resources in time, people, or funding for the strategies. However, an organization's ability to document decisions and recommendations that are linked to divisional priorities may help the leadership allocate and reallocate resources to implement those decisions or forward recommendations for further discussion.

6

IMPLEMENTATION

There are many ways to implement an outcomes-based assessment process. The following suggestions are not meant to be prescriptive; rather, they are meant to serve as guidelines for consideration. When implementing a process at an institution in your own division or a unit in student affairs, three initial steps should always be taken:

1. Clarify the purpose of assessment, including defining the terminology used in the process, developing an explanation of why you are engaging in the process, and determining how you intend the results to be used.
2. Establish a professional development team and training plan that includes educating people about outcomes-based assessment as well as ways to meaningfully engage students in learning and development.
3. Ensure that you have shifted your focus to student learning and development throughout implementation. While evaluating the effectiveness of services is important, if we lose sight of how those services contribute to student success, we may lose sight of the goal of student success.

Clarifying the Purpose

The first step in implementing the assessment process at your institution is to clarify your purpose. Student affairs professionals who are attempting to implement systematic outcomes-based assessment processes often face confusion when identifying who will be using the data generated from the outcomes-based assessment process and how they will be used (Bresciani, in press-a). It is often the case that not all faculty and administrators agree on how the data can be used or even why they should engage in such a systematic evaluation process. Thus, the first step in implementation is to encourage agreement about the answers from throughout the organization to the following questions:

- Why do we want to implement a systematic process of outcomes-based assessment?
- How do we hope to improve student learning as a result of the implementation of this process?
- How do we envision that the data generated from this process will contribute to external accountability indicators and requirements?

To answer these questions, key stakeholders in the organization must respond to a variety of questions, adapted from Bresciani (2006). A submenu of the questions may be taken to the appropriate group of stakeholders where facilitated conversations can be held.

Process Questions
- Why do we want to systematically implement a process for collecting student learning outcomes data?
- What do we hope to accomplish as an institution/division from gathering these data?
- What value does engaging in this process have for me as a faculty member/administrator?
- How will engagement in this process make me a better faculty member/administrator?
- How will engagement in this process improve student learning and/or development?
- How will it improve my program?
- How will it improve academic and student support services?
- How will it improve the reallocation of resources within the institution?
- How will it advance our strategic initiatives?
- What do we want the process to consist of?
- What are the external requirements (e.g., regional accreditor, professional accreditors, state) placed on the process?

- How well does what we envision connect with the external requirements for the process?
- How will my assessment report be reviewed?
- Will someone determine the level of quality of my assessment process?
- What are the consequences for a low level of quality in my assessment process?
- Is there a specific timeline for implementation of this process?
- Will someone do the "regular" data collection (e.g., enrollment figures, retention and graduation rates, budget figures)?
- Will someone coordinate the assessment planning process?
- Will assessment plans be public?
- Will the assessment plans be centrally located?
- Will someone be in charge of documentation?
- How public will my report be?
- Will the assessment reports be centrally located?
- How will this process link with other college planning and reporting efforts?
- How will this process link with institutional planning and reporting efforts?
- Are there institutional learning outcomes that all courses/workshops/projects/programs need to assess?
- What if courses/workshops/projects/programs cannot link their outcomes to specific institutional goals?
- What if I can't link my outcomes to institutional/divisional goals or strategic priorities?
- What happens if I don't turn in an outcomes-based assessment plan?
- What happens if I don't turn in an outcomes-based assessment report?

Data Usage Questions

- What kinds of data do we expect to generate from this process?
- Which data will be used to inform program improvements?
- Which data need to be used to compare our program to other similar programs?
- Which data need to be used to compare our institution to other similar institutions?

- How well will those types of data contribute to what we envision for this process?
- How well will those types of data contribute to what is required externally of this process?
- Will we require programs to report data on outcomes that illustrate how well we are moving toward our divisional/institutional goals or strategic initiatives?
- How will we prioritize resources for outcomes-based informed decisions that are proposed to move toward our divisional/institutional goals or strategic initiatives?
- If data show we are not moving toward our divisional/institutional goals or strategic initiatives, will we revisit the strategic plan that informed them?
- What types of data are required for me to demonstrate how my course/workshop/project/program is contributing to student learning?
- What types of data are required for me to demonstrate my program's accomplishments?
- How often are we required to report these data?
- Who will see the data that are generated from my course/workshop/project/program?
- How will these data be used by others who will see them?
- Will I be able to consult with others on how the data I generate are used?
- Will someone determine the level of quality of my course/workshop/project/program?
- What are the consequences for a low level of quality in my course/workshop/project/program?
- Will groups external to my program be using my data? If so, for what purpose? Will I be able to consult with them on how they use the data?
- Will the results be used to evaluate me personally?
- Will program/departmental/college/division/institutional reallocations be based on the data we produce?
- Will I receive an allocation to improve my program if the data demonstrate that additional funding is necessary to improve the program?

- What happens if data I produce reveal that someone else's program needs to be improved for my program to be improved (e.g., poor performance in composition is affecting my student's ability to write well)?
- How will program review results inform enrollment planning, performance indicators, and other types of evaluation?

The selection of stakeholders who will be asked subsets of these questions depends on the organizational structure and its culture. Committees can be established to examine some aspect of the process or to determine which course of action is most appropriate. For example, Colorado State University student affairs professionals use a

> steering committee to guide assessment efforts for student development outcomes. It forms subcommittees that annually review student affairs assessment plans. Using a common rubric of planning and evaluation standards of best practice, these committee members embed on-line comments into assessment plans to improve outcome descriptions and evaluation methods. The peer review subcommittees involve graduate students from the student affairs master's program to gain their perspective and to advance their development for the workplace. (Bresciani et al., 2009)

Other groups of people to whom these questions may be posed include members of the following:

- Academic/Faculty Senate
- Staff Senate
- President's Cabinet
- Academic Affairs/Instructional Services executive leadership
- Student Affairs/Student Services executive leadership
- Business and Finance executive leadership
- Institutional Research and Planning staff
- Program Review Committee
- Student Learning Outcomes Committee in each unit, if any, and in the campuswide community
- Strategic Planning Committee
- Institutional Curriculum Committee

- General Education Curriculum Committee
- Annual Planning Committee
- Accreditation Preparation Committee
- District/system executive leadership
- District/system Institutional Research and Planning staff
- Student government or other student groups

In addition to these types of groups or committees, conversations may also be encouraged among members of committees and leadership teams that have relationships with organizations external to the college. For example, if institutional leaders feel they must become particularly responsive to an external organization within the community, then it may be helpful to organize conversations within the subset of data usage questions for that group. This can assist with identifying the types of useful data when demonstrating accountability to external constituents.

For example, if neighboring community members want to see a decrease in the number of times they call the police about loud noises from area fraternity and sorority housing, then it is important for those evaluating fraternity and sorority life to be aware of what their neighbors are holding them accountable for. However, if they just use this indicator as the only indicator of student success, then they would be unable to explain to the neighbors the types of learning occurring in their community citizenship programs and how they know it is occurring. Similarly, if the board of trustees is holding student affairs professionals accountable for increased retention rates, then increased retention rates must be used. However, what also must be communicated to trustees are the indicators related to those programmatic initiatives that lead to increased retention, such as evidence of engagement, a student's ability to identify peer pressures, and his or her knowledge of how to seek assistance and from where.

Once conversations are held with members of these individual groups and any other groups that are identified as important participants in these conversations, the responses can be summarized, and initial answers may be formulated to address the following questions:

- Why do we want to implement a systematic process of outcomes-based assessment?
- How do we hope to improve student learning as a result of the implementation of this process?

- How do we hope this information will advance our university/division goals or strategic initiatives?
- How do we envision that the data generated from this process will contribute to external accountability indicators and requirements?

Where responses vary according to groups, key representatives of those groups can be brought together with a facilitator to discuss differences of opinions and ways to resolve those differences.

Once agreement has been reached among all the key stakeholders, the college or university can publish on its Web site (so that it is easily accessible by all) a shared conceptual framework of outcomes-based assessment. Institutions may also want to use a common language that works across disciplines and colleges. In addition, a Frequently Asked Questions and Answers (FAQs) page to address some of these key questions is highly encouraged. Such transparent agreement and succinct answers to typical questions can provide a foundation for the establishment of the systematic outcomes-based assessment process. This transparent agreement typically reduces anxiety for those engaging in the assessment process and it may begin to build trust in the process. Much of the confusion inherent, and therefore resulting mistrust, in the process stems from misunderstanding what the process is, why it is important, and how the data will be used and by whom (Bresciani, 2006; Palomba & Banta, 1999; Suskie, 2004).

Professional Development

If consideration for professional development is not taken into account, implementation of outcomes-based assessment can be a challenging process. Many scholars have discussed the importance of providing a professional development framework for outcomes-based assessment for faculty and student affairs practitioners to understand its real purpose: to improve the underperforming student using a systematic, reflective process (Banta & Associates, 2002; Maki, 2004; Palomba & Banta, 1999; Suskie, 2004). Additionally, Bresciani (in press-c) discovered that professional development for outcomes-based assessment must also be accompanied by professional development in student learning and development theories to make the entire assessment process effective, efficient, and enduring.

Thus, one of the initial steps in implementing a systematic outcomes-based assessment process involves implementing and evaluating a professional development sequence. The professional development sequence, in essence, "trains" faculty and practitioners to examine the manner in which they plan, deliver, and evaluate their courses, curriculum, and academic and student support services. The sequence models the *retraining and retooling* philosophy employed commonly in industry. For example, when an organization has found it needs to provide updated training to staff to bring the staff up to speed with the latest industry standards and the most efficient ways of doing business, the organization can take a step back and plan the most effective training methods. In the case of this proposed implementation plan, the faculty and student affairs practitioners can be released from their day-to-day duties at different times in the implementation process to learn how to plan and apply the most recent research in student development and learning theories, evaluation/assessment, and/or collaborative planning and implementation strategies. For example, officials at Paradise Valley Community College stated,

> the commitment to provide up front professional development for student affairs professionals to become grounded in the contemporary literature that supports the premise of student learning outside of the classroom as a valued part of the students' total college experience was essential. (Bresciani et al., 2009)

Once professional development is in place, outcomes-based assessment program review data are collected. Following this step, professional development of faculty and practitioners continues; however, the bulk of the educational efforts are geared toward midlevel administrators and managers as they will be collecting outcomes, findings, and decisions provided by faculty and practitioners. During this professional development strategy, training may be needed to help decision makers examine the data in a manner that leads to the prioritization and funding of division or institutional strategic initiatives. In addition, such professionals can be taught how to use these data to inform accountability conversations by explaining the meaning behind performance indicators such as retention rates, graduation rates, transfer rates, and time to degree.

In the next part of the implementation stage, a meta-assessment process is involved. Implementing a meta-assessment to determine how well you are truly changing the nature of your student-learning-centered culture through the implementation of outcomes-based assessment is essential. Meta-assessment is important whether you choose to follow the suggestions in this book precisely or choose to modify them in accordance with your organizational culture. As a part of this meta-assessment process, the professional development component is evaluated for its effectiveness, as is the extent to which data generated from the outcomes-based assessment program review process have improved student learning and development. The question of whether the evaluation process (e.g., outcomes-based assessment program review) is sustainable over time and whether the decisions resulting from the process were worth investing resources in the process is the focal point of chapter 7.

The Professional Development Plan

To prepare each unit adequately for the successful adoption of an outcomes-based assessment program review, professional development is essential. As administrators at Texas A&M University stated,

> strongly consider the creation of a training module for participants to attend before the project is used widely across the university. The training session can be used to create a common starting point through its ability to introduce participants to the history of the project, the goals and desires of the project, and lastly create tools and methods of feedback for the advisors and supervisors to use. Training can also be used to create a basic rhythm across the campus upon which departments, divisions, and colleges can add their music establishing a commonality for students to share with each other. Simply stated, training can be used to create a sense of identity for learning outcomes across the University. (Bresciani et al., 2009)

A training schedule should be presented to each college, division, or unit depending on how large an initiative you are undertaking. Each unit can provide one primary contact to organize and facilitate the training schedule at that person's institution. The primary contact's role and responsibilities can include the following, any of which may be delegated to other members of the division practitioners but not without the direct supervision of the primary contact:

- Work with key division and/or institutional leadership to establish the core training team for the division (this team, sized appropriately for each division, can serve as the training team for the rest of the members of the division).

- Examine the training schedule and each training module's content and in consultation with key personnel at the institution and within the division (e.g., institutional assessment coordinator), determine appropriate modifications for each unit.
- Schedule workshop times and advertise workshops.
- Arrange facilities, refreshments, and prepare materials for the workshop.
- Coordinate workshop evaluations with the division or institutional assessment coordinator or the division primary contact.
- Serve as a consultant for follow-up train-the-trainer workshops.

Key faculty and administrators who are willing to complete the full cycle of training can be appointed by appropriate unit personnel. The primary contact can serve as the coordinator of this team. Members of this team serve as the core trainers for disseminated learning so they will be able to train others. In this manner, a train-the-trainer model is implemented. While membership numbers and areas represented on this team may vary in accordance with institutional culture, the division staff are encouraged to have the following representation on this training team to ensure understanding of terms and processes across organizational reporting lines:

- Academic/Faculty Senate representative
- General Education Committee member
- Institutional assessment/student learning outcome (SLO) coordinator
- Division Assessment/SLO coordinator
- Program review coordinator
- Campus master plan/strategic plan coordinator
- Two practitioners at large, representing disciplines not in the previous makeup
- Undergraduate student representative
- Graduate student representative

If professional development is implemented at a smaller level, such as in a department within a division, then it is important that divisional representatives are of an authority level and knowledge level that are representative of the division as a whole. In other words, it is not as important to have one member from each department within a division if that is not possible. It is important, however, to make sure that a member of the training committee who is representing a department but is not a member of that department is able to speak with authority when he or she returns to that department to train its members.

The role and responsibilities of this training team include:

- Examining each training module's content in consultation with institutional and divisional key personnel, including the primary contact for the division's professional development; determining appropriate modifications for the subtraining area (e.g., units).
- Determining the schedule and training makeup for each subtraining area in consultation with the primary campus contact. (Depending on each division's culture, the subareas for training will be determined. For example, all residence life professionals may come together for training in one division, while another combines all professionals responsible for building community into one training area.)
- Scheduling workshop times and advertising the workshops.
- Arranging facilities and refreshments and preparing materials for the workshop.
- Coordinating workshop evaluations with the division or institutional assessment coordinator or division primary contact.

One copy of all training materials may be provided to each participating unit electronically so that each department can disseminate the materials according to its needs. A sample training schedule follows:

Year One
  1. Overview of assessment, which shall include
     a. shared conceptual framework for assessment
     b. common language
     c. purpose of assessment
     d. describing how data will be used
     e. drafting an assessment plan
     f. writing outcomes

g. concept mapping

h. introduction to evaluation methods and criteria

Materials produced from this session include program assessment plans and concept maps. The common elements of an outcomes-based assessment plan are detailed and each is explained fully in chapter 3.

2. Selecting appropriate evaluation methods for assessment and analyzing data, which shall include

a. questions to consider when selecting evaluation methods

b. writing rubrics and criteria checklists

c. implementing and using surveys, portfolio assessment, standardized tests, and published instruments

d. using and interpreting benchmarks and other performance indicators

e. interpreting data to inform decisions for improvement

f. interpreting data to explain institutional performance indicators

g. identifying priorities for improvement and funding allocations

Materials produced from this session include refined program assessment plans and concept maps, as well as tools and criteria for evaluation. Evaluation methods and criteria are more fully explored in chapter 4.

3. Overview of application of theories in student learning and development, which can include

a. characteristics of effective program designs

b. various types of effective pedagogy and training models

c. illustrations of effective means to evaluate learning and development

d. consideration of affective or noncognitive characteristics that contribute to enhanced student learning

e. consideration of models for academic student support

f. explorations of models that generate comparable data

Materials produced from this session include refined program assessment plans and concept maps. In addition, refinement of program planning and refinements in or new plans for proposed interventions for academic support and student support services may also be produced as a result of this workshop session.

Year Two

1. Repeat of Year One for those who may need it or who are new to the division
2. Interpreting data to inform meaningful decisions
   a. interpreting data to inform decisions for improvement, part 2
   b. interpreting data to explain institutional performance indicators
   c. identifying priorities for improvement and funding allocations
   d. determining what to do with "bad" data
   e. determining refinements necessary in the assessment plan
   f. reporting your results, decisions, and recommendations
   g. aligning SLO assessment plan results with program review, strategic initiatives, and institutional values

   Materials produced from this session include refined program assessment plans and reports as well as refined concept maps, program plans, and other program materials. Use of data to inform decisions is addressed in more detail in chapter 5.

3. Addressing concerns of implementation, which shall include
   a. involving students in the process
   b. rolling up program-level data for use with state and institutional indicators
   c. challenges in using assessment data for decision making, including challenges in prioritizing decisions and funding for improvements
   d. refining the plan to assess
   e. addressing barriers to assessment

   Materials produced from this session include refined assessment process documents, program assessment plans and reports, as well as refined concept maps, program plans, and other program materials, in addition to programmatic evidence of improved student learning and development. Common barriers and strategies to address them are more fully explored in chapter 8.

Year Three

1. Repeat of Year One and Year Two for those who may need it or who are new to the division
2. Conducting a meta-assessment of the process, which shall include
   a. document analysis of assessment plans
   b. identifying your needs to improve the process

    c. encouraging more involvement in the assessment of student learning and development

    d. aligning reporting processes with one another and reducing paperwork

    e. addressing sustainability of the process

    f. addressing additional educational/training needs

Materials produced from this session include refined assessment process documents, planning and reporting processes, and discussions of how the institution is transforming as a result of using outcomes-based assessment. Meta-assessment is discussed more thoroughly in chapter 7.

3. Overview of electronic solutions for assessment, which shall include

    a. examples to electronically store and retrieve assessment plans and reports

    b. electronically linking data collected in courses/workshops to data collected by programs

    c. using data extracts from transactional systems to interpret outcomes met

    d. using data extracted from systemwide surveys or other databases to interpret outcomes met

    e. discerning when to request a research study versus conducting a refined assessment

Materials produced from this session include refined plans and recommendations for technological processes and systems. Chapter 11 further addresses these topics.

Shifting the Focus to Student Learning and Development

In some cases, conversations or professional development may be required to assist student affairs practitioners in their shift to evaluating student learning and development rather than only evaluating service effectiveness. Even though student affairs practitioners may recognize the value of evaluating student learning and development, they may still need some assistance in reflecting on how they contribute directly or indirectly to student learning and development. The following questions, which were formulated through conversations with James A. Anderson, president of Fayetteville State University, may assist practitioners as they move toward reflecting on how they contribute to student learning and development:

- What do you expect your students to know and be able to do by the end of their education at your institution?
- What do the curricula and the cocurricula add up to?
- What do you do in your programs to promote the kinds of learning and development that your institution seeks?
- Which students benefit from which cocurricular experiences?
- What cocurricular processes are responsible for the intended student outcomes the institution seeks?
- How can you help students make connections between classroom learning and experiences outside the classroom?
- How do you intentionally build upon what each of you fosters to achieve?
- What is the thinking task, intellectual experience, and/or cocurricular experience that needs to be designed relative to the preparation level and diversity of the students at your institution?
- Can the interpersonal transactions that occur in the everyday life of the student that reflect cultural orientations serve as a basis for potential new models of critical thinking? What curricular experiences will promote this skill development?
- What structures need to evolve to ensure that students have the opportunity to enhance an academic self-concept and understand their role in the culture of learning at your institution?
- How are you interpreting the input variables of your students in order to provide them with the necessary academic and student support?
- How are you programmatically contributing to student engagement and therefore contributing to academic success?
- How are you contributing to the provision of a physical environment that contributes to student success?
- How are you contributing to meeting all the needs students have before they can begin to learn?
- How are you directly or indirectly contributing to student learning?
- How are you directly or indirectly supporting student learning?
- How are you directly or indirectly interfering with student learning?

If further reflection is needed, the SLI (American College Personnel Association, 1994) offers some rich examples of additional reflection questions. In addition, chapter 9 presents examples and ideas for consideration when collaborating with faculty to promote these conversations.

If practitioners still find it challenging to identify how they contribute to student learning and development, they should consider the following suggestions. When student affairs professionals feel the farthest away from contributing to students' learning and development directly or indirectly, remind them that they do play a crucial role. These professionals can consider how providing quality services and responsiveness to service requests allows for the student to spend less time on logistical concerns and more time on his or her own contributions to student success. In addition, the professionals may want to consider how clearly their information for basic needed services is provided and how quickly and easily it can be accessed. Finally, these professionals often have great insight into how policy and practice may be improved as they typically field multiple complaints and concerns from students. Use of data gathered through outcomes-based assessment can mean a better understanding of purpose for the organization. A better understanding of purpose can contribute to empowerment of the professionals to offer ideas for improvement, particularly when they see the goals of the organization reinforced through decision making.

7

CRITERIA FOR EVALUATING EFFECTIVE OUTCOMES-BASED ASSESSMENT PRACTICE

To ensure that assessment is not a process for the sake of the process, it is helpful to engage student affairs practitioners in two conversations. The first conversation invites them to envision how they want their institution to look once they have fully taken on outcomes-based assessment or evidence-based decision-making processes. In this conversation, practitioners identify criteria that will assist them in acknowledging that outcomes-based assessment will contribute to public recognition of the value to their day-to-day activities. The criteria identified and defined will help the practitioners describe how they have transformed their culture into one that is student-learning centered and one that demonstrates continuous improvement practices to advance the success of students.

The second conversation encourages practitioners to identify criteria that aid them in understanding how well they are engaged in the inquiry process. These criteria serve as a set of guidelines for systematic practice and moves them toward making their institution become a student-learning-centered organization that embodies evidence-based decision making. These sets of criteria often focus on the details of what constitutes a good assessment plan, report, and process while the preceding set of criteria examines the organization as a whole. To further illustrate these two different conversations, specific examples will be discussed in the paragraphs that follow and the chapter will commence with suggestions for the creation of such criteria.

Steps in Creating the Criteria

Regardless of whether you identify criteria that aid practitioners in understanding how well they are engaged in the inquiry process or you define the criteria that describe how student-learning centered your organization is, certain steps can assist you with the formation of each. The first step is to create a task force or committee that effectively represents the units within your division. Chapter 6 contains questions for formulating a committee or a task force that will serve to design a shared conceptual framework and common language. The same sets of questions asked when establishing a conceptual framework can also be used when forming a team to create criteria to audit the overall assessment process. It is important to involve those individuals who are advocates of the assessment process as well as those who are not. The variety of perspectives represented from both sides of the spectrum are what lend themselves to a rich discussion and thorough consideration of all relevant criteria.

Once the committee or task force is formed, ensure that the assignment for the team is clear. The focus of the committee should be based on one of two charges: (a) creating criteria to help practitioners identify whether they have completed a well-thought-out assessment plan and report, or (b) creating criteria that will allow institution or division administrators to find out if their organization is a student-learning-centered organization that fully embodies evidence-based decision making. As such, committee or task force membership may need to vary based upon its charge.

Questions to consider that aid practitioners in understanding how well they are engaged in the inquiry process based on their plans and reports can be found on p. 107. The importance of asking and answering these questions stems from the belief that engagement in outcomes-based assessment must be systematic; however, that does not mean it must be void of reflection. In an effort to standardize the process, some institutions make the mistake of creating templates that limit the inquiry process and the flexibility needed by various units in regard to their work flow.

For example, when North Carolina State University administrators first rolled out the expectation for assessment among their academic and student support services professionals, they realized that the assessment report deadline of June 1 did not work at all for the professionals who worked in orientation and for those who worked in the summer bridge transition programs.

Thus, the deadline for those reports had to be changed to better coincide with work flow. Similarly, they also realized that a June 1 deadline was not feasible for the learning communities professionals, as the faculty they needed to consult with to analyze data and make decisions were not available in the summer. Furthermore, the template provided did not allow them to document collaboratively designed outcomes and results.

Thus, criteria used to evaluate assessment plans and reports can assist practitioners with understanding what is required; however, we must ensure that what we require is not gathered in a manner that thwarts intrinsic intellectual curiosity. The following questions are intended to keep this from happening as you design your criteria for evaluating assessment plans and reports.

1. Why do we require what we require in the assessment plan/report?
2. Do our criteria clearly state what we want reported in a manner that is effective, efficient, yet reflective of a quality inquiry process?
3. Are our criteria applicable to all types of units within our division?
4. Do the proposed criteria assist in the development of more reflective planning and reporting of outcomes-based assessment?
5. Are the criteria based on good practice?
6. Do the criteria limit creativity?
7. Do the criteria promote thoughtful reflection and inquiry?
8. Do the criteria contribute to a culture centered around student learning?
9. Do the criteria promote a culture of evidence-based decision making?

Similar questions are posed when creating criteria for identifying how well we have implemented outcomes-based assessment. However, an additional set of questions to consider include several of those in chapter 6, as well as the following questions.

1. What do we want our organization to look like once we have successfully implemented systematic outcomes-based assessment?
2. How will the quality of student learning and development be enhanced by the process?
3. How will the quality of intentional planning and purposeful reflection be enhanced?

4. What qualities or characteristics do we hope to identify in service provision and in all our business processes?

5. What qualities or characteristics do we hope to identify in the way we prioritize the implementation of action plans that deliver the intended outcomes?

6. What division or institutional qualities or characteristics do we hope to identify in the way we prioritize allocations and reallocations of funds and other resources to improve our programs, services, and student learning and development?

7. What division or institutional qualities or characteristics do we hope to identify in the way we refine personnel evaluation processes?

8. What division or institutional qualities or characteristics do we hope to identify in the way we prioritize and plan professional development activities?

9. What division or institutional qualities or characteristics do we hope to identify in the way we prioritize and inform strategic initiatives?

10. What division or institutional qualities or characteristics do we hope to identify in our collaborations within the division and across the university/college?

11. What division or institutional qualities or characteristics do we hope to identify in the way we interact and communicate with each other within the division and across the university/college?

12. What division or institutional qualities or characteristics do we hope to identify in the way we interact with students, parents, and other constituents?

13. How transparent is our decision-making process?

14. How transparent are our outcomes and decisions?

15. How do we know that time invested in this process is worth the improvement brought about by the process?

Plan and Report Criteria

When providing professional development for practitioners with regard to how to engage in outcomes-based assessment, it is extremely helpful to provide the practitioners with guidelines about what is expected in the process (Bresciani, 2006; Bresciani et al., 2004; Maki, 2004; Palomba & Banta, 1999;

Suskie, 2004). Such guidelines can help eliminate distrust about the process and clarify what is asked from practitioners.

As discussed in chapter 3, the details that make up the components of an assessment plan and report can be formulated by a division or institutional assessment committee. Each component of the plan and report can be listed; however, the criteria often determine whether quality inquiry has occurred that provide the specific ideas of how to improve assessment processes. Such feedback leads to improvements in the information and the processes that collect that information.

When creating the guidelines and criteria, various institutional professionals may approach the provision of each in a variety of different ways. Some prefer to provide a template that simply lists the needed components and provides brief descriptions of what those components are. In an effort to ensure everyone involved in the process understands the template, further professional development or a more detailed handbook explaining what should be incorporated in the template may be required. Some institutions provide criteria checklists such as the one in Table 2 to assist practitioners with the reflective process of completing the assessment plan and its template.

In Table 2, adapted from Bresciani and Sabourin (2002), the criteria focus primarily on what is contained in the assessment plan and report rather than the process derived to create such a plan and report. An individual could pose these questions to himself or herself once having completed the assessment plan or report to determine whether what was written is representative of a quality assessment process. Such questions cause reflection about the completion of a required template rather than just filling in the boxes, so to speak, of a required document.

Moving Toward Criteria for the Process

The following excerpts from good-practice institutions emphasize the need to provide criteria for the assessment process. In their assessment reports, many institutions highlight the changes suggested for the assessment process itself as well as for the programs. Paradise Valley Community College (2007) administrators require practitioners to answer the question, "What changes did you suggest and/or implement as a result of this assessment?" Officials at Texas A&M University (2005) ask, "How is your organization planning

TABLE 2
Meta-Assessment Criteria Checklist

	Yes	No
Department or Program Mission		
1. Does the department's or program's mission clearly link to the university's mission statement?	Y	N
2. Does the department's or program's mission clearly link to the division's or unit's mission?	Y	N
Department or Program Goals		
1. Do the goals of the department or program clearly link to the mission statement?	Y	N
2. Are the goals of the department or program a broad and general statement of what the program wants students to be able to know and to do?	Y	N
3. Do the goals of the department or program represent the primary values of the department or program?	Y	N
4. Do the goals of the department or program align with institutional, system, state, professional standards, or accreditation goals, if appropriate?	Y	N
Learning Outcomes		
1. Does each outcome (program, student learning, student development, faculty development, and practitioners' development) reflect a substantial aspect of the program or department goals?	Y	N
2. Does each outcome describe what the program or department intends for students and/or practitioners to know (cognitive), think (affective, attitudinal), or do (behavioral, performance, psychomotor)?	Y	N
3. Collectively, do the outcomes reflect the most important purposes of the program?	Y	N
4. Is each intended outcome:		
a. detailed and specific?	Y	N
b. appropriate to the program or department?	Y	N
c. measurable/identifiable?	Y	N
d. meaningful in making decisions on how to improve the program?	Y	N
5. Does the program have a component to be able to deliver/implement each outcome?	Y	N
Evaluation Methods and Implementation of Assessment		
1. Are multiple methods, if appropriate, used to assess outcomes?	Y	N
2. Do the assessment methods include direct and indirect measures of outcomes?	Y	N
3. Is each assessment method or tool appropriate to the outcome it is evaluating?	Y	N
4. Are comparison data used where possible?	Y	N
5. Do the proposed methods of assessment appear feasible in terms of design, time, and resources?	Y	N

	Yes	No
6. Do the proposed methods of assessment yield information that is suitable for making decisions about program or department improvement?	Y	N
7. Are the proposed methods of assessment consistent with the best-accepted practices in that profession?	Y	N
8. Are criteria identified for each method?	Y	N
9. Are these criteria realistic?	Y	N
10. Where possible, are the proposed evaluation methods incorporated in the day-to-day operation of the program?	Y	N
11. Is the proposed evaluation method appropriate for the manner in which the outcome is delivered?	Y	N
12. Are institutional indicators, such as retention rates and graduation rates, included where appropriate to do so?	Y	N

Results

	Yes	No
1. Do the results reflect a discussion on the manner in which students were sampled?	Y	N
2. Is appropriate information from results shared with multiple audiences?	Y	N
3. Is there enough detail or specificity to determine the extent to which the outcomes have been achieved?	Y	N
4. Do the results inform decisions for program improvement?	Y	N
5. Do the results explain how they can be used for comparison, if at all?	Y	N
6. Has a process for verifying or authenticating the results been discussed?	Y	N

Decisions and Recommendations

	Yes	No
1. Is the use of the results adequately stated to explain the specific changes made as a result of assessment?	Y	N
2. Do the decisions and recommendations posed clearly align with the results of the assessment?	Y	N
3. Do the decisions and recommendations posed clearly align with the outcome that was assessed?	Y	N
4. Is there evidence that assessment will be ongoing/continuous?	Y	N
5. Are decisions made about improving the intended delivery of the outcomes?	Y	N
6. If recommendations are made, is it clear to whom the recommendations have been given and why?	Y	N
7. Are decisions made to improve the assessment process, including the refinement of outcomes or criteria?	Y	N
8. Have decisions been prioritized according to division/institutional goals or strategic initiatives?	Y	N
9. Have resources been allocated or reallocated to fund the improvements?	Y	N

Note. From "Criteria Checklist for an Assessment Program," by M. J. Bresciani and C. M. Sabourin, 2002, *National Association for Student Personnel Administrators, Inc NetResults E-Zine.* Adapted with permission.

to use the data for improvement? What decisions will you be making based on this assessment?" Finally, Colorado State University staff (2004) request practitioners to list what "changes or progress since last formal and/or strategic review?" When information such as this is requested, it is important that these institutions' criteria or assessment plan/report templates reflect that this type of information is necessary for the practitioners to be considered as engaging in quality assessment practice.

In addition, some institutions require the reporting of specific types of decisions, such as data that informed the decisions regarding allocation and reallocation of resources. Good-practice institutions report identifying how the assessment process will help with budget decisions. Northern Arizona University (2007) officials specifically ask, "How will the results of this project help in making [division name] budget decisions?" Similarly, Colorado State University (2004) staff require unit practitioners to discuss in two pages the nature of "Financial Support and Efficiency" and to "provide a self analysis of cost effectiveness and qualities of services provided."

Another way to encourage reflection about assessment plans and reports is to urge individuals to think about what they have written in the report as well as reflect on the process that contributed to what is written. Many good-practice institutions not only provide criteria to practitioners to help them complete assessment plans and reports in a quality manner, but they also provide criteria to encourage a quality overall process.

Many good-practice institutions inquire about the nature of collaborative efforts, which includes faculty participation. Paradise Valley Community College (2007) representatives look for "faculty members who participated in [the] assessment." Colorado State University (2004) officials seek to examine the extent to which collaborative efforts exist within and among the "Division of Student Affairs, other University departments, other state agencies and other community groups."

While not a common practice, the authors found this interesting and chose to include it: Paradise Valley Community College (2007) staff request that practitioners report on how their understanding of assessment was enhanced. They specifically ask their practitioners, "How has your understanding of and involvement in assessment been enhanced this year?" Such feedback provides them with information on how to improve their professional development plan as well as inform refinements for the overall process.

In a similar manner, when requesting information about how to improve the process, some institutions ask for feedback about the challenges that practitioners faced implementing assessment. Paradise Valley Community College (2007) officials specifically request information on how the assessment process had been limited over the past year and inquires about the "description of necessary changes and strategies contemplated to effect changes [in the process itself]." Colorado State University (2004) staff ask for a "description of any problems associated with the structure."

Some institutions have incorporated criteria for evaluating the assessment plan and report as well as the process used in the creation of the plan and report. Table 3 illustrates such an example.

Process Criteria for Meta-Assessment

To implement an outcomes-based assessment process and not evaluate it could be considered hypocritical. Establishing the criteria for determining how you know your assessment process is creating the culture you intended for it to create or to reinforce is most important for the organization (Bresciani, 2006; Maki, 2004; Palomba & Banta, 1999; Suskie, 2004). As mentioned previously, determining the criteria for identifying how your organizational members will know they are reaching their intended goals is extremely important. In other words, can members of your organization articulate how they will know their institution has become a learning organization, one that uses evidence-based decision making to inform decisions that promote student success? This is an important question to answer; therefore, writing the evaluation plan of the assessment process is necessary (Bresciani, 2006). Outlining short-range and long-range goals of the assessment process and evaluating the success of those goals through outcomes-based assessment models the dynamic nature of the inquiry process itself.

To assist with the creation of the criteria for the meta-assessment process, Table 4 illustrates some criteria for determining if you have effective, efficient, and enduring evidence-based procedures in place. The criteria in this rubric, intended for any organization to consider and adapt, use the meta-assessment work of several assessment scholars (Eckel, Green, & Hill, 2001; Ewell, 1997; López, 2002; Maki, 2001; Palomba & Banta, 1999).

TABLE 3
Analytic Rubric for Assessing JFKU[a] Annual Learning Results

Criterion	Initial	Emerging	Developed	Highly Developed
Assessable Outcomes (PLOs[b]) & Criteria	PLO statements exist but do not identify what students can do to demonstrate learning. (Statements such as "Students understand major theories" do not specify how understanding can be demonstrated and assessed.)	Some of the outcomes (PLOs) indicate how students can demonstrate their learning. Action verbs may be general and some PLOs may not be observable/ measurable. Criteria for assessing each outcome are not identified, are incomplete, are vague, or are not observable/measurable.	The PLOs describe how students can demonstrate learning, identifying observable/measurable results (e.g., "Graduates can describe and compare psychospiritual theories & techniques" or "Students can establish, maintain, evaluate and utilize the therapeutic relationship to serve the mental health needs of the client"). Criteria are articulated for each PLO, though some may need refining to be clear and measurable.	The PLOs clearly describe how students can demonstrate learning; this includes clearly distinguishing between what the program wants students to know (cognitive), ways students think (affective/attitudinal), or what students should be able to do (behavioral, performance, psychomotor). Criteria for assessing each PLO are clearly articulated, capture the most important dimensions of student learning for each PLO, and include descriptions of student performance at varying levels of mastery for each criterion (e.g., rubric).
Evidence & Methods	It is not clear that potentially valid evidence for each relevant outcome is collected *and/or* individual faculty use idiosyncratic criteria to assess student work or performances.	Faculty have reached general agreement on the types of evidence to be collected for each outcome; they may not have aligned the evidence with relevant or clearly articulated criteria.	Faculty collect relevant & sufficient evidence for each outcome, including at least one line of direct evidence. Instruments used (e.g., rubrics) assess the level of student attainment of each outcome. Results are compiled and analyzed annually.	Assessment criteria, such as rubrics, have been pilot-tested and refined over time; they usually are shared with students. Self-assessment and feedback from external reviewers has led to refinements in the assessment process, and the department uses external benchmarking data.
Reliable Results	Reviewers are not calibrated to apply assessment criteria in the same way; there are no checks for inter-rater reliability.	Reviewers are calibrated to apply assessment criteria in the same way *or* faculty routinely check for inter-rater reliability.	Reviewers are calibrated to apply assessment criteria in the same way, *and* faculty routinely check for inter-rater reliability.	Reviewers are calibrated, and faculty routinely find assessment data have high inter-rater reliability.

Presentation & Analysis of Results	Results (data table or other means) are not included in report. Report identifies some conclusions or implications of results, but no explanation of how these claims are derived from results. No reasoning offered in support of claims. Follow-up improvements may or may not be identified.	Results (data table or other means) are included but unclear or missing key data. Report identifies some conclusions and implications of results, but the claims are vague or questionably related to results. Some albeit insufficient reasoning offered in support of claims. Questions of validity or reliability of results are not discussed. Follow-up improvements identified but connection to results is unclear.	Results (data table or other means) are clearly delineated for each line of evidence, indicating both the raw numbers and percentages of student achievement. Report clearly articulates conclusions and implications which could be drawn from results, including a consideration of reliability and validity of results. May offer vague or insufficient reasons/explanations to support some of the claims. Explicitly connects suggested improvements to relevant results.	Results (data table or other means) are clearly delineated for each line of evidence, indicating both the raw numbers and percentages of student achievement at various levels of mastery. Report articulates a well-reasoned critique of probable conclusions and implications which could be drawn from the results. Results are analyzed in relation to levels of mastery. Includes a well-reasoned discussion of validity and reliability of results. Identifies improvements for student learning and/or for program assessment practices. Explicitly connects suggested improvements to relevant results.
Results Are Used	Results for each outcome may or may not be collected. They are not discussed among faculty.	Results for each outcome are collected and may be discussed by the faculty, but results have not been used to improve the program or proposed changes do not clearly follow from results.	Results for each outcome are collected, discussed by faculty, analyzed, and used for program planning and improvement. Proposed changes follow directly from results.	Faculty routinely discuss results, plan needed changes, secure necessary resources, and implement changes. They may collaborate with others, such as librarians or student affairs professionals, to improve results. Follow-up studies confirm that changes have improved learning.

Note. From *Analytic Rubric for Assessing Annual Learning Results* by Cyd Jenefsky and the JFKU Program Review Council (2008). Adapted in part from *WASC[c] rubrics* (2007) and Bresciani and Allen (2002). Reprinted with permission of the author.

[a]John F. Kennedy University
[b]Program Learning Outcomes
[c]Western Association of Schools and Colleges

TABLE 4
Meta-Assessment Rubric A Rubric to Evaluate the Overall Assessment Process

	Exemplary	Developing	Beginning
Shared Purpose			
Common Language	Articulate the level of understanding of the common language document through self-report surveys, interviews, and document analyses of assessment plans.	Articulate some level of understanding of the common language document through self-report surveys, interviews, and document analyses of assessment plans.	Articulate no level of understanding of the common language document.
Conceptual Understanding	Articulate the level of understanding of the Shared Conceptual Understanding document through self-report surveys, interviews, and document analyses of assessment plans.	Articulate some level of understanding of the Shared Conceptual Understanding document through self-report surveys, interviews, and document analyses of assessment plans.	Articulate no level of understanding of the Shared Conceptual Understanding document.
Student Learning	Demonstrate the extent to which assessment is used to improve student learning.	Demonstrate some extent to which assessment is used to improve student learning.	Does not demonstrate an extent to which assessment is used to improve student learning.
Teaching	Demonstrate the extent to which assessment is used to improve teaching.	Demonstrate some extent to which assessment is used to improve teaching.	Does not demonstrate an extent to which assessment is used to improve teaching.
Assessment Plans	All academic and co-curricular programs have complete assessment plans.	Some academic and co-curricular programs have complete assessment plans.	No academic and co-curricular programs have complete assessment plans.
Faculty's Innate Intellectual Curiosity	Demonstrate that faculty's participation in assessment is based on innate intellectual curiosity or is intrinsically motivated.	Demonstrate to some extent that faculty's participation in assessment is based on innate intellectual curiosity or is intrinsically motivated.	Unable to demonstrate that faculty's participation in assessment is based on innate intellectual curiosity or is intrinsically motivated.

Criterion			
Administrator's Innate Intellectual Curiosity	Demonstrate that administrator's participation in assessment is based on innate intellectual curiosity or is intrinsically motivated.	Demonstrate to some extent that faculty's participation in assessment is based on innate intellectual curiosity or is intrinsically motivated.	Unable to demonstrate that administrator's participation in assessment is based on innate intellectual curiosity or is intrinsically motivated.
Using the Results	Results from the assessment process are used to inform discussions, decisions, and recommendations.	Results from the assessment process are somewhat used to inform discussions, decisions, and recommendations.	Results from the assessment process are not used to inform discussions, decisions, and recommendations.
Expectation of Student Learning	Explicit statements regarding the institution's expectations for student learning are widely publicized.	Some statements regarding the institution's expectations for student learning are publicized.	None of the statements regarding the institution's expectations for student learning are publicized.
Expectation of Student Learning Assessment	Explicit statements regarding the institution's expectations for the evaluation of student learning are widely publicized.	Some statements regarding the institution's expectations for the evaluation of student learning are publicized.	None of the statements regarding the institution's expectations for the evaluation of student learning are publicized.

Collaboration Across the Institution

Criterion			
Collaboration	Demonstrate that Colleges, Student Affairs, and other academic and student support programs work together to promote assessment efforts.	Somewhat demonstrate that Colleges, Student Affairs, and other academic and student support work together to promote assessment efforts.	Does not demonstrate that Colleges, Student Affairs, and other academic and student support are working together to promote assessment efforts.
Flexibility	There is flexibility in the process, so that each program can maintain its autonomy and unique definition of meaning through assessment.	There is some flexibility in the process, so that each program can maintain its autonomy and unique definition of meaning through assessment	There is no flexibility in the process, so that each program can maintain its autonomy and unique definition of meaning through assessment.
Shared Resources	Demonstrate that assessment resources are shared across Colleges and Divisions.	Demonstrate that some assessment resources are shared across Colleges and Divisions.	Unable to demonstrate that assessment resources are shared across Colleges and Divisions.

TABLE 4 (Continued)

	Exemplary	Developing	Beginning
Rituals, Practices, Symbols			
Annual Awards	Annually present an award for Excellence in Assessment that improves student learning.	Nominated for an award for Excellence in Assessment that improves student learning.	Not eligible for an award for Excellence in Assessment that improves student learning.
Accomplishments	Sponsoring of an annual quality assessment conference where faculty and administrators have an opportunity to showcase their assessment accomplishments.	There is some sponsoring to develop a quality assessment conference where faculty and administrators have an opportunity to showcase their assessment accomplishments.	There is no sponsoring of a quality assessment conference where faculty and administrators have an opportunity to showcase their assessment accomplishments.
Program Documentation	There is systematic use of the chosen assessment management software or other documentation tools such as Word, Excel, the Web, etc.	There is some use of the chosen assessment management software or other documentation tools such as Word, Excel, the Web, etc.	There is no documentation collected for use in the chosen assessment management software or other documentation tools such as Word, Excel, the Web, etc.
University Documentation	Creation and use of an institutional electronic portfolio web site, where annual and bi-annual assessment plans and results are posted on program web sites, yet it links to one central web site.	Some creation and use of an institutional electronic portfolio web site, where annual and bi-annual assessment plans and results are posted on program web sites, yet it links to one central web site.	Have no documentation collection for creation and/or use of an institutional electronic portfolio web site, where annual and bi-annual assessment plans and results are posted on program web sites, yet it links to one central web site.
Participation	There is 100% participation/response by programs to the university's assessment requests.	There is 50% participation/response by programs to the university's assessment requests.	There is 0% participation/response by programs to the university's assessment requests.

Leadership Commitment

Using the Results	Results from the assessment process are used to inform discussions, decisions, and recommendations.	Results from the assessment process are somewhat used to inform discussions, decisions, and recommendations.	Results from the assessment process are not used to inform discussions, decisions, and recommendations.
Evidence for Reward	Engagement in the assessment process is recognized and/or rewarded.	Engagement in the assessment process is somewhat recognized and/or nominated for reward.	There is no engagement in the assessment process to be recognized and/or rewarded.
Administrator Resources (Annual Allocation)	Senior administrators annually provide resources for the assessment process.	Senior administrators annually provide some resources for the assessment process.	Senior administrators annually provide no resources for the assessment process.
Administrator Resources (Additional Allocation)	Senior administrators provide additional resources to enhance assessment practices and improve faculty and practitioners' understanding of assessment process and use of assessment results.	Senior administrators provide some additional resources to enhance assessment practices and improve faculty and practitioners' understanding of assessment process and use of assessment results.	Senior administrators provide no additional resources to enhance assessment practices and improve faculty and practitioners' understanding of assessment process and use of assessment results.
Administrator Resources (Special Projects)	Senior administrators regularly provide resources for special projects to enhance the assessment process (e.g., pilot projects, summer stipends, departmental grants, and support for professional development).	Senior administrators periodically provide resources for special projects to enhance the assessment process (e.g., pilot projects, summer stipends, departmental grants, and support for professional development).	Senior administrators regularly do not provide resources for special projects to enhance the assessment process (e.g., pilot projects, summer stipends, departmental grants, and support for professional development).
Faculty Resources (Annual Allocation)	Faculty leaders annually provide resources for the assessment process.	Faculty leaders annually provide a few resources for the assessment process.	Faculty leaders annually provide no resources for the assessment process.
Faculty Resources (Additional Allocation)	Faculty leaders provide additional resources to enhance assessment practices and improve faculty and practitioners' understanding of assessment process and use of assessment results.	Faculty leaders provide additional resources to enhance assessment practices and improve faculty and practitioners' understanding of assessment process and use of assessment results.	Faculty leaders provide additional resources to enhance assessment practices and improve faculty and practitioners' understanding of assessment process and use of assessment results.

TABLE 4 (Continued)

	Exemplary	Developing	Beginning
Leadership Commitment (Cont.)			
Faculty Resources (Special Projects)	Faculty leaders regularly provide resources for special projects to enhance the assessment process (e.g., pilot projects, summer stipends, departmental grants, and support for professional development).	Faculty leaders infrequently provide resources for special projects to enhance the assessment process (e.g., pilot projects, summer stipends, departmental grants, and support for professional development).	Faculty leaders do not provide resources for special projects to enhance the assessment process (e.g., pilot projects, summer stipends, departmental grants, and support for professional development).
Administrator's Authorization	Senior administrators routinely authorize various campus offices (e.g., institutional research) to provide the support services needed to carry out the assessment process.	Senior administrators infrequently authorize various campus offices (e.g., institutional research) to provide the support services needed to carry out the assessment process.	Senior administrators do not authorize various campus offices (e.g., institutional research) to provide the support services needed to carry out the assessment process.
Faculty Authorization	Faculty leaders routinely authorize various campus offices (e.g., institutional research) to provide the support services needed to carry out the assessment programs.	Faculty leaders infrequently authorize various campus offices (e.g., institutional research) to provide the support services needed to carry out the assessment programs.	Faculty leaders do not authorize various campus offices (e.g., institutional research) to provide the support services needed to carry out the assessment programs.
Balance	There is balance between administrative and faculty leadership.	There is a growing attempt for balance between administrative and faculty leadership.	There is no balance between administrative and faculty leadership.
Faculty Advocates	Faculty leaders advocate the continual improvement of student learning as an institutional priority.	Faculty leaders somewhat advocate the continual improvement of student learning as an institutional priority.	Faculty leaders do not advocate the continual improvement of student learning as an institutional priority.

Criterion			
Administrator Advocates	Administrative leaders advocate the continual improvement of student learning as an institutional priority.	Administrative leaders somewhat advocate the continual improvement of student learning as an institutional priority.	Administrative leaders do not advocate the continual improvement of student learning as an institutional priority.
Reward and Recognition			
Participation	Faculty and administrators participate in the annual assessment conference.	Faculty and administrators infrequently participate in the annual assessment conference.	Faculty and administrators do not participate in the annual assessment conference.
Publications	There are a number of publications and presentations on assessment.	There are some publications and presentations on assessment.	There are no publications and presentations on assessment.
Awards	There are Awards given for achievement in assessment that improves student learning and development.	There are Awards given for achievement in assessment that improves student learning and development.	There are no Awards given for achievement in assessment that improves student learning and development.
Use of Results	Results from the assessment process are used to inform discussions, decisions, and recommendations.	Results from the assessment process are somewhat used to inform discussions, decisions, and recommendations.	Results from the assessment process are not used to inform discussions, decisions, and recommendations.
Recognition (on the Web)	Faculty and/or practitioners' achievements in assessment are showcased on-line.	Faculty and/or practitioners are making achievements in assessment showcased on-line.	Faculty and/or practitioners have no achievements in assessment showcased on-line.
Recognition (other)	Administrators' achievements in assessment are showcased in other ways.	Administrators making achievements in assessment in other ways.	Administrators have no achievements in assessment in other ways.
Celebrations	The institution publicly and regularly celebrates what it has learned about student learning, performance, and achievement through assessment.	The institution regularly celebrates, sometimes publicly, what it has learned about student learning, performance, and achievement through assessment.	The institution does not publicly and regularly celebrate what it has learned about student learning, performance, and achievement through assessment.

TABLE 4 (Continued)

	Exemplary	Developing	Beginning
Reward and Recognition (Cont.)			
Promotion and Tenure	Assessment practices and research are used in promotion and tenure decisions.	Assessment practices and research are sometimes used in promotion and tenure decisions.	Assessment practices and research are not used in promotion and tenure decisions.
Education and Support			
Evaluation of Assessment	All assessment plans are evaluated as exemplary given the criteria articulated on the Bresciani & Allen rubric and feedback on those assessment plans is given to the faculty.	Some assessment plans are evaluated as exemplary given the criteria articulated on the Bresciani & Allen rubric and feedback on those assessment plans is given to the faculty.	No assessment plans are to be evaluated as exemplary.
Participation	100% Attendance of faculty and administration to assessment workshops.	50% Attendance of faculty and administration to assessment workshops.	0% Attendance of faculty and administration to assessment workshops.
Assessment Resource Website	The website is used.	Learning how to use the website.	The website is not used.
Use of Results—Planning	We are able to link planning to assessment.	We are trying to link planning to assessment.	We are unable to link planning to assessment.
Use of Results—Budgeting	We are able to link budgeting to assessment.	We are trying to link budgeting to assessment.	We are unable to link budgeting to assessment.
Administrator's Responsiveness	There is high responsiveness from administrators to faculty and/or practitioners' needs and concerns for assessment.	There is moderate responsiveness from administrators to faculty and/or practitioners' needs and concerns for assessment.	There is little responsiveness from administrators to faculty and/or practitioners' needs and concerns for assessment.

	High	Moderate	Little
Faculty Responsiveness	There is high responsiveness from administrators to faculty and/or practitioners' needs and concerns for assessment.	There is moderate responsiveness from administrators to faculty and/or practitioners' needs and concerns for assessment.	There is little responsiveness from administrators to faculty and/or practitioners' needs and concerns for assessment.
Budget	A budget line has been established and sufficient resources are allocated annually in order to sustain a comprehensive assessment program.	Plan to establish a budget line and allocate sufficient resources annually in order to sustain a comprehensive assessment program. Special request money is used to support assessment initiatives.	No plans for a budget line to be established or sufficient resources allocated annually in order to sustain a comprehensive assessment program.
Funding	Funds are available and sufficient to support consultation, workshops, and professional development for faculty and practitioners in the area of assessment of student learning and teaching.	Some funds are available to support consultation, workshops, and professional development for faculty and practitioners in the area of assessment of student learning and teaching.	Funds are unavailable and non-sufficient to support consultation, workshops, and professional development for faculty and practitioners in the area of assessment of student learning and teaching.
Budget for Improvements	Administrators and key faculty are given the responsibility and authority to use budgeted resources to support academic and co-curricular changes based on assessment findings.	Administrators and key faculty have some responsibility and authority to use budgeted resources to support academic and co-curricular changes based on assessment findings.	Administrators and key faculty are not given the responsibility and authority to use budgeted resources to support academic and co-curricular changes based on assessment findings.
Assessment Resource Website Label	The web site is perceived to be of great help in understanding assessment.	The web site is perceived to be of some help in understanding assessment.	The web site is not perceived to be helpful in understanding assessment.
Information	Information about assessment activities and their results are communicated regularly to the campus community.	Information about assessment activities and their results are communicated infrequently to the campus community.	Information about assessment activities and their results are not communicated regularly to the campus community.
Allocation of Resources	The institution systematically and routinely links assessment results to the allocation of resources for the improvement of student learning.	The institution infrequently links assessment results to the allocation of resources for the improvement of student learning.	The institution has not systematically and routinely linked assessment results to the allocation of resources for the improvement of student learning.

TABLE 4 (Continued)

	Exemplary	Developing	Beginning
Depth and Pervasiveness			
Faculty Engagement	Faculty members systematically engage in effective assessment.	Faculty members engage in effective assessment sometimes.	Faculty members do not engage in effective assessment.
Faculty Collaboration	Faculty members routinely collaborate to determine appropriate measures for program outcomes and to justify and recommend improvements based on results.	Faculty members infrequently collaborate to determine appropriate measures for program outcomes and to justify and recommend improvements based on results.	Faculty members do not collaborate to determine appropriate measures for program outcomes and to justify and recommend improvements based on results.
Faculty Support	Faculty members speak both publicly and privately in support of assessment.	Faculty members support assessment but do not speak out in public.	Faculty members do not support assessment.
Faculty Education	Faculty members systematically educate persons unfamiliar with institutional and program assessment about the value of assessment.	Faculty members infrequently educate persons unfamiliar with institutional and program assessment about the value of assessment.	Faculty members do not systematically educate persons unfamiliar with institutional and program assessment about the value of assessment.
Faculty Exploration	Faculty members continually explore the uses of assessment in the context of research on learning theories, and active learning strategies.	Faculty members infrequently explore the uses of assessment in the context of research on learning theories, and active learning strategies.	Faculty members do not continually explore the uses of assessment in the context of research on learning theories, and active learning strategies.

Criteria			
Faculty Use of Results	Faculty members routinely link their results from the assessment process and use them to inform discussions, decisions, and recommendations.	Faculty members infrequently link their assessment results from the assessment process and use them to inform discussions, decisions, and recommendations.	Faculty members don't have any assessment results from the assessment process and use them to inform discussions, decisions, and recommendations.
Administrator's Engagement	Administrators systematically engage in effective assessment.	Administrators engage in effective assessment sometimes.	Administrators do not engage in effective assessment.
Administrator's Collaboration	Administrators routinely collaborate to determine appropriate measures program outcomes and to justify and recommend improvements based on results.	Administrators infrequently collaborate to determine appropriate measures program outcomes and to justify and recommend improvements based on results.	Administrators do not routinely collaborate to determine appropriate measures program outcomes and to justify and recommend improvements based on results.
Administrator's Support	Administrators speak both publicly and privately in support of assessment.	Administrators support assessment.	Administrators do not support assessment.
Administrator's Education	Administrators systematically educate persons unfamiliar with institutional and program assessment programs about the value of assessment.	Administrators infrequently educate persons unfamiliar with institutional and program assessment programs about the value of assessment.	Administrators do not systematically educate persons unfamiliar with institutional and program assessment programs about the value of assessment.
Administrator's Exploration	Administrators continually explore the uses of assessment in the context of research on learning theories, and active learning strategies.	Administrators infrequently explore the uses of assessment in the context of research on learning theories, and active learning strategies.	Administrators do not explore the uses of assessment in the context of research on learning theories, and active learning strategies.
Administrator's Use of Results	Administrators routinely link their assessment results from the assessment process and use them to inform discussions, decisions, and recommendations.	Administrators infrequently link their assessment results from the assessment process and use them to inform discussions, decisions, and recommendations.	Administrators do not link their assessment results from the assessment process and use them to inform discussions, decisions, and recommendations.

TABLE 4 (Continued)

	Exemplary	Developing	Beginning
Depth and Pervasiveness (Cont.)			
Student Involvement	Throughout their academic and co-curricular programs, students are systematically provided occasions to reflect upon their academic and co-curricular work, in oral and written forms, about the levels of success they think they have experienced in achieving the learning outcomes articulated by faculty.	Throughout their academic and co-curricular programs, students are sometimes provided occasions to reflect upon their academic and co-curricular work, in oral and written forms, about the levels of success they think they have experienced in achieving the learning outcomes articulated by faculty.	Throughout their academic and co-curricular programs, students are not provided occasions to reflect upon their academic and co-curricular work, in oral and written forms, about the levels of success they think they have experienced in achieving the learning outcomes articulated by faculty.
Sustainability			
Characteristics	All of the aforementioned characteristics are met.	Some of the aforementioned characteristics are met.	None of the aforementioned characteristics are met.
Student Learning	Academic and co-curricular units and programs consider assessment of student learning to be integral to their educational and research operations.	Academic and co-curricular units and programs consider assessment of student learning to be somewhat important to their educational and research operations.	Academic and co-curricular units and programs do not consider assessment of student learning to be integral to their educational and research operations.
Flexibility	There is flexibility in the process, so that each program can maintain its autonomy and unique definition of meaning through assessment.	There is some flexibility in the process, so that each program can maintain its autonomy and unique definition of meaning through assessment.	There is no flexibility in the process, so that each program can maintain its autonomy and unique definition of meaning through assessment.

Continuous Improvement	Academic and co-curricular units and programs regard assessment findings as essential for continuous improvement of their program offerings.	Academic and co-curricular units and programs regard assessment findings as helpful but not integral knowledge essential for continuous improvement of their program offerings.	Academic and co-curricular units and programs do not regard assessment findings as helpful or integral of knowledge essential for continuous improvement of their program offerings.
Diversity	There is great diversity of the process.	There is some diversity of the process.	There is no diversity of the process.
Documentation	The institution maintains a system of data collection and documentation of the entire assessment process, which helps sustain an effective assessment program.	The institution maintains data collection and documentation of the entire assessment process, which sustains an effective assessment program but it is not systematic.	The institution does not maintain a system of data collection and documentation of the entire assessment process, which helps sustain an effective assessment program.
Meta-Analysis	The comprehensive assessment program is evaluated regularly and is modified as necessary for maximum effectiveness.	The comprehensive assessment program is evaluated somewhat and is modified as necessary for maximum effectiveness.	The comprehensive assessment program is not evaluated regularly and is modified as necessary for maximum effectiveness.
Program Evaluation	Institutional and departmental assessment programs are annually reviewed and updated.	Institutional and departmental assessment programs are infrequently reviewed and updated.	Institutional and departmental assessment programs are not reviewed and updated.
Evaluation of Decisions Made	The effectiveness of the changes made to curriculum, academic and co-curricular resources, and support services from assessment results are evaluated and documented.	Changes are made in curriculum, academic and co-curricular resources, and support services from assessment results but those changes are not evaluated.	No changes are made in curriculum, academic and co-curricular resources, and support services from assessment results.

TABLE 4 (Continued)

	Exemplary	Developing	Beginning
Sustainability (Cont.)			
Resources	The institution provides financial resources and other support for all aspects of the assessment process, including assisting and writing meaningful and manageable outcomes, research and evaluation design, data collection and maintenance, interpretation, and decision-making, and consultation services and assistance with systematic documentation.	The institution provides some financial resources and other support for all aspects of the assessment process, including assisting and writing meaningful and manageable outcomes, research and evaluation design, data collection and maintenance, interpretation, and decision-making, and consultation services and assistance with systematic documentation.	The institution provides no financial resources and other support for all aspects of the assessment process, including assisting and writing meaningful and manageable outcomes, research and evaluation design, data collection and maintenance, interpretation, and decision-making, and consultation services and assistance with systematic documentation.
Documentation	The institution maintains a system of data collection and documentation of the entire assessment process, which helps sustain an effective assessment program.	The institution maintains data collection and documentation of the entire assessment process, which sustains an effective assessment program but it is not systematic.	The institution does not maintain a system of data collection and documentation of the entire assessment process, which helps sustain an effective assessment program.
Student Learning	Student learning is central to the mission of the institution.	Student learning is growing towards being central to the mission of the institution.	Student learning is not central to the mission of the institution.
Culture of Evidence	A "culture of evidence-based decision-making" has emerged, sustained by a faculty and administrative commitment to excellent teaching and effective learning.	Working towards a "culture of evidence-based decision-making", to be sustained by a faculty and administrative commitment to excellent teaching and effective learning.	A "culture of evidence-based decision-making" has not yet emerged, to be sustained by a faculty and administrative commitment to excellent teaching and effective learning.

New Hires	All new hires (administrators and faculty) demonstrate a commitment to assessment and if not, are trained in assessment.	Some new hires (administrators and faculty) demonstrate a commitment to assessment and if not, are trained in assessment.	No new hires (administrators and faculty) demonstrate a commitment to assessment.
Methodology/Process	The methodology and process used for assessment fits the operation, needs, and resources of the program employing the process.	The methodology and process used for assessment sort of fits the operation, needs, and resources of the program employing the process.	The methodology and process used for assessment does not fit the operation, needs, and resources of the program employing the process.
Faculty/Expert Designed	The assessment process, while institutionally expected and supported, is faculty/expert designed.	The assessment process, while institutionally expected and supported, is somewhat faculty/expert designed.	The assessment process, while institutionally expected and supported, is not faculty/expert designed.
Priorities Made Clear	The priorities of the institution are made clear as decisions and resources to support those decisions are informed by outcomes-based assessment processes.	Some institutional priorities are made clear as decisions and resources to support those decisions are informed occasionally by the outcomes-based assessment process.	Information from the outcomes-based assessment process is not used to inform decisions or resource allocation as related to institutional priorities.
Personnel Evaluation	Personnel evaluation processes reflect the priorities of the institutions and faculty and practitioners are rewarded for improving what the institution values.	Personnel evaluations sometimes reflect institutional priorities and faculty and practitioners are occasionally rewarded for improving what the institution values.	Personnel evaluations do not reflect institutional priorities and faculty and practitioners are not rewarded for improving what the institution values.

Note. Designed by Bresciani, M. J., & Jacovec, L. M., using the work of Eckel, Green, & Hill, 2001; Ewell, 1997; López, 2002; Maki, 2001; Palomba & Banta, 1999. From "Meta-analysis Rubric" by M. J. Bresciani and L. M. Jacovec (n.d.).

Applying the Criteria

The purpose of this chapter is to provide suggestions for designing criteria that guide reflection about institutional/divisional assessment and reporting processes. The intent is not to promote institutional/divisional assessment practices for the sake of assessment but to stimulate thought about designing processes that improve student learning and development and the overall culture of evidence-based decision making (Bresciani, 2006; Maki, 2004; Palomba & Banta, 1999; Suskie, 2004). Through encouraging a meta-assessment process, we intend to embody what Senge (1990) refers to as a *learning organization.*

After creating the criteria and before implementing a meta-assessment process or before providing simple feedback on unit assessment plans and reports, we recommend considering the following:

1. It is important to emphasize that the purpose of the criteria and the evaluation of the plans and reports is to further the process of reflection about how student success can be improved, not to determine whether a unit is doing quality work. (Determining whether a unit is doing the quality of work it should is not typically the job of the team that provides the professional development and review of the quality assessment process. However, many of the ideas contained in this chapter can be applicable to the separate process of reviewing the actual quality of work produced by a unit.)

2. It is important to provide practitioners with the criteria you are using to evaluate their assessment plans and/or reports prior to asking them to complete the plans and reports.

3. Once you have reviewed the plans and reports, it is important to provide feedback that will encourage practitioners to consider what is best for their students and their units. For example, providing feedback in the form of questions posed may encourage additional reflection from the practitioners about how they can best fit the given advice into their unit's needs.

4. When suggesting improvement in the assessment process, it is important to provide specific examples to illustrate good practice and realization of the criteria.

5. It is important to rotate membership of the committee providing the feedback to increase professional development and shared responsibilities for the culture of improvement.

6. It is important to keep the process criteria and the manner in which feedback is given transparent. This does not mean that you have to make public the actual feedback for any given unit. Rather, it means that everyone is aware of what happens when good assessment is not completed.

7. It is important to continue to remind everyone of the purpose of outcomes-based assessment—to improve student success—so that the manner in which the process is improved does not become all consuming, rendering the purpose for it—improving student learning and development—meaningless.

8. Finally, it is important to have fun! It is a privilege to do the work we get to do, and the evaluation of it, which informs intentional planning and additional purposeful reflection, should be as inspiring as actually doing the work.

PART THREE

BARRIERS, RESOURCES, AND FUTURE CONSIDERATIONS

8

BARRIERS TO
EFFECTIVE ASSESSMENT

Outcomes-based assessment in student affairs has been in existence for quite some time (Banta & Associates, 2002; Bresciani, 2006; Upcraft & Schuh, 1996). While student affairs as a profession has access to research about how well the programs that typically fall within divisions of student affairs contribute to overall student success (Astin, 1993; Hurtado, Engberg, & Ponjuan, 2003; Kuh, Kinzie, Schuh, Whitt, & Associates, 2005; Mentkowski & Associates, 2000; National Research Council, 2001; Pascarella, 2006; Pascarella & Terenzini, 2005; Tinto, Love, & Russo, 1993), many student affairs' programs have been overlooked for their specific contributions to student learning and development at their institutions (Bensimon, 2007). Thus, more recently, student affairs professionals have begun to evaluate their contributions to student learning and development in a more systematic manner. However, even with the increased emphasis on evaluating student learning and development, many student affairs professionals are still without evidence of their contributions.

In some instances where student affairs professionals are not engaged in outcomes-based assessment, they have simply become overwhelmed by the common barriers that result when implementing outcomes-based assessment. Research illustrates the common barriers to implementing outcomes-based assessment, and many of them may be applicable to student affairs professionals.

Common Barriers to Implementing Outcomes-Based Assessment

The reasons faculty and administrators do not pervasively and systematically engage in outcomes-based assessment are often (a) a lack of time, (b) a lack of resources, and (c) a lack of understanding of assessment (Banta & Associ-ates, 2002; Bresciani, 2006; Bresciani et al., 2004; Palomba & Banta, 1999; Suskie, 2004; Upcraft & Schuh, 1996). In addition to these well-documented barriers, student affairs professionals have been known to have a few addi-tional primary barriers: (a) a lack of understanding the student learning and development theory that undergirds their practice; (b) a lack of collaboration within and across their divisions to extend to faculty members; and (c) a disconnect between what the student affairs professionals expect students to be able to know and do, and the manner in which student affairs profession-als are actually able to provide the opportunity for the outcome to be realized (Bresciani, in press-c).

Grounded theory analysis of the case studies that informed writing this book introduced two categories that have not been discussed at great length in previous literature. This chapter describes the barriers that the student affairs professionals experienced at their institutions. In addition, the strate-gies they employed to overcome those barriers are also discussed, even though the details of those strategies have been introduced in earlier chapters.

Findings Particular to These Cases

Each of the members in this study faced numerous barriers when imple-menting outcomes-based assessment in their student affairs divisions. The barriers discovered during open coding were similar to those reported in pre-vious studies (Bresciani, 2006; Maki, 2004; Palomba & Banta, 1999; Suskie, 2004; Upcraft & Schuh, 1996). When looking at how barriers were addressed, the ways in which professionals were able to overcome barriers were described in more detail than the barriers themselves. This means either that when members of an organization encounter a barrier, they have to be prepared with several strategies to address the barrier, or that once members of an institution overcome many of their barriers, they simply cannot recall them in detail.

Regardless, Table 5 outlines the categories of barriers that emerged through open, axial, and selective coding (Strauss & Corbin, 1990) of the participants' case studies. The properties column provides more description of the category.

TABLE 5
Open Coding of Barriers in Student Affairs Assessment

Principle Theme	Category	Properties
Barriers	Time	competing priorities; added responsibility; unsure how to reallocate responsibilities; a feeling of being overwhelmed when trying to approach doing this
	Resources	professional development; time; rewards for engaging in outcomes-based assessment
	Knowledge and skills	do not know what assessment is or how to do it; do not know how to compose outcomes; do not know how to select and implement evaluation methods; anxiety over not knowing creates more anxiety
	Coordination of process	no central person to coordinate division efforts or to coordinate committee
	Conceptual framework for assessment	having to overcome traditional and/or historical definitions of assessment; addressing student affairs' role in assessing student learning and development; unclear connection of process to academic processes and accreditation processes; unclear expectations for engaging in assessment
	Collaboration with faculty	faculty do not collaborate with student affairs staff and vice versa; faculty involvement is limited
	Trust	varying levels of conceptual understanding for assessment across various levels of leadership; varying expectations across various levels of leadership; how will evidence be used? who will see evidence? varying degree of expectations for role of student affairs professionals in evaluating student learning and development
	Managing expectations	acknowledging what the goals of a program may be versus (a) how a program can actually deliver those goals, (b) the capacity of the practitioners to deliver the goals, (c) the knowledge of the practitioners to be able to deliver those goals, (d) therefore determining what the actual outcomes really are; clarifying the difference between passion for what the outcomes should be and what they really can be

Representatives from institutions participating in this study reported common barriers to implementing outcomes-based assessment. Descriptions of many of these barriers have already been widely published (Banta & Associates, 2002; Bresciani, 2006; Bresciani et al., 2004; Palomba & Banta, 1999; Suskie, 2004; Upcraft & Schuh, 1996). Thus, this chapter focuses on summarizing the strategies used to address the barriers.

Before illustrating some of these strategies, another open-coding table (see Table 6) describes the strategies identified in these case studies. Using open, axial, and selective coding of the case studies, the categories in Table 6 emerged. The properties column provides more description of the category.

While the open-coding tables provide helpful information in understanding the types of barriers addressed and the strategies used to address them, other chapters in this book incorporate the narrative and examples of how to address these barriers, particularly chapters 5, 6, 7, and 9. The two strategies, which are not fully discussed in other chapters but are included in Table 6 include "Celebrate" and "Be flexible."

Through outcomes-based assessment, we can demonstrate the significant contributions that cocurricular experiences have on student learning and development. As such, these contributions should be celebrated as opposed to being looked at as one more task to complete. At Oregon State University "finding joy in assessment and celebrat[ing] successes" has "helped to sustain the assessment efforts particularly when the hurdles seemed overwhelming" (Bresciani et al., in press). Paradise Valley Community College provides annual awards, including the Assessment Cup, which "was somewhat skeptically received [in the beginning, but] it has proven to be a cherished and sought after distinction" (Bresciani et al., 2009). Other suggestions include highlighting assessment results in an annual report or regularly sharing results at department or division meetings.

Incorporating assessment into everyday practice is not something that happens overnight at any institution. Developing a culture of assessment is something that takes time and flexibility. At CSUS,

> it took most of the directors about six months to determine the appropriate balance of program improvement and student learning and then to write all of the objectives or outcomes in ways that were SMART—specific, measurable, aggressive yet attainable, results-oriented, and timely. (Bresciani et al., 2009)

As determining balance often takes time, one strategy identified by the institutions contributing to this book is flexibility. North Carolina State University officials specifically suggest to "not be afraid to make changes throughout the process, and embrace creative ideas and strategies. People like to see that you are responsive to their needs" (Bresciani et al., 2009). The

TABLE 6
Open Coding of Strategies to Overcome Barriers in Student Affairs Assessment

Principle Theme	Category	Properties
Strategies	Educate	create a professional development plan; provide workshops and one-on-one consultations; read the literature; send student affairs practitioners to workshops and conferences; ground the practice in theory; bring in consultants; use others' ideas; share what works and what doesn't work with each other
	Clarify	provide a conceptual framework, common language, and a template for student affairs practitioners to use when compiling assessment plans and reports; clarify expectations for engagement in the process; consider writing the expectation into position descriptions; clarify expectations for excellence
	Collaborate	across the division with colleagues; outside the division with faculty; involve students, when appropriate; involve community members, when appropriate; connect outcomes with each other
	Coordinate	develop a plan for how you will implement and support the assessment efforts in your division; hire someone to coordinate the process; create an assessment committee with representatives from each department as well as faculty and possibly students; determine whether departmental committees are appropriate; provide retreats to plan implementation steps and expectations; provide summer sessions to discuss results and examine how well the process is working; discuss findings and decisions at division meetings; at division meetings, determine what else is needed to support the process; incorporate assessment into strategic planning and program review; ask individuals to relate their outcomes to division and institutional goals and learning outcomes
	Celebrate	encourage engagement in the process; acknowledge contributions; provide incentives; incorporate results into assessment or end-of-year report
	Be flexible	create a flexible timeline, paying attention to workloads of varying offices; balance structure with needed flexibility; be ready to adjust anything in the process to make it work well
	Keep it simple	evaluate a small number of outcomes each year; don't try to assess everything you do even if you have a multiple-year assessment plan; don't try to achieve your ideal immediately

following section details how these strategies, along with the strategies discussed in other chapters (particularly chapter 5), align with the barriers that institutions identified.

Findings to Consider

It is interesting to note that in most instances when case study participants described their barriers, they described the strategies they used to overcome those barriers. While some institution members report having overcome many of their barriers, others report they are still struggling with some of them.

To understand how the strategies aligned with the barriers, we matched the categories of barriers to strategies. Table 7 illustrates that matching. Notice, however, that two categories of barriers, *managing expectations* and *trust*, were not directly addressed with strategies. Using research related to these areas (Bresciani, in press-c; Bresciani, 2006; Maki, 2004; Palomba & Banta, 1999; Suskie, 2004; Upcraft & Schuh, 1996), we propose strategies for managing expectations and trust not found in these case studies but found in other research (Bresciani, 2006).

TABLE 7
Matched Strategies and Barriers

Barriers	*Strategies*
Knowledge and skills	Educate, clarify, coordinate
Resources	Educate, clarify, coordinate
Conceptual framework for assessment	Educate, clarify
Resources	Educate, celebrate, clarify
Collaboration with faculty	Collaborate, educate, clarify
Coordination of process	Coordinate, educate
Time	Coordinate, collaborate, educate, be flexible, keep it simple
Trust	Celebrate, clarify, educate
Managing expectations	Educate, clarify, collaborate, coordinate

Trust

The issue of trust can be found in two primary areas. The first area is the inability to trust student affairs professionals with the work of contributing to and evaluating student learning and development. The second area, and a common trust issue for faculty as well, is with regard to the use of the data. These barriers and strategies to address them are also covered in chapters 5 and 9. As we continue, let us examine the first area: the inability to trust student affairs professionals with the work of contributing to and evaluating student learning and development.

Case study participants described, in essence, scenarios with their leadership, either faculty leadership or administrative leadership, that seemed to influence their ability to evaluate student learning and development fully. Some of the scenarios, such as those on pp. 156–157 in chapter 9, insinuated that student affairs professionals were perceived to have little to no role in evaluating student learning and development. Education, first and foremost of the student affairs professionals, and second of their faculty colleagues, could begin to alleviate this misconception.

For example, if student affairs professionals are grounded in the theory that informs their practice, as well as grounded in the manner they effectively practice their work (Bresciani, in press-c), they may be more able to theoretically articulate their contributions to student learning and development. Therefore, student affairs professionals will be able to accurately describe their contribution to student learning and development as they move to evaluate that student learning and development. As a result, the colleagues who plan the curriculum and cocurriculum can begin to trust the student affairs professionals' expertise as it will be made evident in planning and evaluation.

The second key area of trust is also one of the key sustainability concerns for all who engage in outcomes-based assessment. Expectations of leadership vary on how and to what extent the results are used (Bresciani, 2006; Maki, 2004). This is often a very real barrier for many practitioners and faculty. What we learned from earlier research is that outcomes-based assessment is not sustainable as a process to transform an institution into a learning-centered institution unless the leadership supports the engagement in that process and does so in a consistent manner; this includes the use of data derived from the process to inform decisions (Bresciani, 2006; Maki, 2004).

It is important to remember to make the process of how data will be used to inform decisions and who will use the data for decisions as public as possible. Doing so will begin to reduce anxiety and demonstrate evidence of consistent behavior. Only over time, through consistent behavior, will trust be established. Chapter 6 provides examples of how to make the process as transparent as possible.

Another aspect of addressing issues of trust is to recognize that no institution, regardless of how affluent it may be, can honor the funding requests for all needed improvements. Therefore, it is important for funding requests to be prioritized in accordance with institutional or divisional values. Making these institutional or divisional values publicly known can assist faculty and administrators alike with the alignment of their program outcomes to these values. Once program outcomes are aligned to values, assessment of the outcomes can take place. Finally, resources to finance the decisions to improve those institutional/divisional values can be prioritized as well.

Addressing issues of trust often involves leadership commitment to the process, leadership commitment to the transparency of how decisions are made, and leadership commitment to the values that inform the prioritization of the allocation and reallocation of resources to improve student success. If you are in a division whose institutional administrators are not committed to assessment, but you want your division committed to assessment, then these same principles can apply to the authority that you have in your level of leadership in the hierarchy. The same could be true if you are a departmental director in a division whose leadership is not committed to outcomes-based assessment. However, keep in mind, that you may be limited by your circle of influence.

For example, as director of a unit, you are the highest level of leader in your organization, and you can clarify how results will be used and to what extent the results will be shared. Yet, be realistic in communicating that you may be unsure how your boss will use the results. If you are the senior officer in your division, then you can provide the type of clarification that is needed, but you may not be able to say how your boss will use the information generated from outcomes-based assessment. Failure to provide clarification on the extent to which engagement in assessment is expected, how results will be used, and who will see the results may breed mistrust.

The ability to focus on your locus of control can help clarify issues of trust and empower practitioners to see where they have the ability to influence interpretation of data, process, and policy and where they do not. The act of simply acknowledging that fact can demystify the process for many and encourage others to engage in the process with clarity of expectations. Focusing on one's own locus of control or circle of influence leads us to the next category that emerged as a barrier but with few suggested alternatives to address it.

Managing Expectations

According to Palomba and Banta (1999), Bresciani et al. (2004), and Bresciani (2006), one purpose of assessment is that it provides an institution's leadership with data to help manage expectations about what can be accomplished with given resources. The same type of management of expectations needs to be considered when planning to engage in outcomes-based assessment. In this we mean that frustration often arises for student affairs professionals when they cannot distinguish between the passion that drives the reason they do what they do from what they can reasonably accomplish given their resources and means of delivery.

Many of this study's participants describe the value of using outcomes to clarify end results for programs, yet some student affairs professionals do not want to let go of the values that inspire their work and therefore confuse those values for outcomes. For example, a residence hall director may want all the residents to take responsibility for their wellness. The director's desire for the students to take responsibility for their own behavior, especially when making choices for their well-being, is exactly why the director loves the job. However, the director is able to distinguish that value from the reality that the only systematic circle of influence he or she has on the resident advisers is when they are in the 2-week training program prior to the start of school and when the director reaffirms that training twice a month in 2-hour meetings. Because the director knows that he or she can only provide training for these students, the director may not actually be able to influence the rest of the residents, unless there are systematic means designed to do so. Thus, the director's outcomes for well-being will be for the resident advisers for the 2-week training programs and for the two 2-hour training sessions per month that follow. It is in these training programs/sessions that the director has a circle of influence on the advisers and where he or she can design systematic ways to deliver and evaluate the expected learning. While retaining the value of well-being for the student body as a whole, the director will only be assessing this set of students in these sets of learning opportunities.

Accepting the reality that what we truly value may not be measurable because we do not actually have programs to influence the outcomes of what we value is a very challenging aspect for student affairs professionals to accept. For people who are truly motivated to change peoples' lives and who know they do so on a daily basis, the inability to systematically evaluate that contribution is frustrating. However, if we keep in mind that the primary purpose of outcomes-based assessment is to establish a systematic process that reveals results that can be used to improve student learning and development, then we can better understand that we do not need to let go of our values to assess what we are able to really deliver.

Thus, the barrier of managing expectations is often addressed through educating student affairs professionals about the difference between the passion that gives them purpose and the identifiable end results they can systematically deliver and therefore systematically evaluate. A further example of this is that while student affairs professionals value changing students' behavior to make healthier choices, the intended outcome is not changed behavior. To actually evaluate the success of your program based on how well you can change behavior means you are trying to influence variables that are outside your locus of control. Rather consider evaluating how well your program contributes the (a) knowledge, (b) skills, and (c) attitudes that precede behavior change.

Recommendations

In closing, it may be helpful to summarize primary considerations when addressing barriers encountered during the implementation of outcomes-based assessment. Many of the following recommendations are summarized from case study participants (see chapters 3, 5, 6), and reiterated in other literature (Banta & Associates, 2002; Bresciani, 2006; Bresciani et al., 2004; Maki, 2004; Palomba & Banta, 1999; Suskie, 2004).

- At every point possible, remind everyone involved with the process what outcomes-based assessment is and what it is not. See chapters 1 and 2 for clarification.
- Do not make assessment a process for process's sake. No one has time for that.

- Address every barrier as if it were the first time you heard it. Show all people respect, and listen to make sure that what they are saying is actually what they are experiencing. Often people express one barrier, such as "I have no time," when another one is underlying it: "My boss will not allow me to reallocate any of my activities for evaluating them." Take the time to find out what is truly expressed.
- Use ideas from others, including the examples in this book, but be sure to adapt the ideas to your own culture. As the authors will attest, if you just pick something up and attempt to adopt it without adapting it to your organizational culture, it may not have the desired effect.
- Reallocate time to the entire process. Every part of this process requires time. Engage in serious discussions about what has to be done versus what items can be reallocated to assessment. For those student affairs professionals who primarily manage crisis situations, be creative about how you can provide them some protected time to engage in outcomes-based assessment, such as scheduling time for reflection and writing it on their calendar. The process of reflection brings about great renewal, and those typically dealing with crisis situations benefit greatly from having scheduled reflection time.
- Find ways to educate, coordinate, and collaborate on improving student learning and development, which includes engaging in meaningful and manageable outcomes-based assessment. Be creative in the ways you integrate required reporting and planning documents to leverage time for practitioners to converse about what did and could happen rather than spending their time writing about it.
- Stay committed to educating, coordinating, and collaborating. Education is a process and so is building the relationships that allow coordination and collaboration to occur. Do not assume that once you have offered instruction on something everyone has it down. Consider creative ways to continue everyone's education, including using train-the-trainer models and fishbowl exercises. Continuing to offer educational support throughout all aspects of the process will alleviate anxiety that may feed upon itself and heighten fear of failure.
- Be clear in communicating your expectations about every aspect of engaging in outcomes-based assessment, from answering questions such as, What happens if I do not do outcomes-based assessment? to

clarifying expectations of who will see the results and how they will be used.

- Focus on your locus of control. Managing our own expectations of how we can contribute to student learning and development in a 1-hour workshop versus a year of continued professional development with our paraprofessionals is important to distinguish. Furthermore, making sure that we maintain the values that give our work meaning while separating what we really can manage to deliver and evaluate is an important distinction to make.

- Find ways to reward the improvement of student learning and development that are informed by outcomes-based assessment results. If you celebrate improvements in student learning and development, professionals may better understand that you are not celebrating a process for the sake of the process but affirming the essence of why their positions exist: to contribute to students' success.

- Balance structure with flexibility. Structure is required to demonstrate that the organization is systematically and continuously engaged in improving student learning and development. However, too much structure causes the process to lose meaning. Paying attention to evaluating what you are asking for and why while examining what promotes professionals' ability to systematically engage in the improvement of student learning and development via outcomes-based assessment promotes a win-win scenario.

- Keep it simple. Remind student affairs professionals that outcomes-based assessment is not research. It is a systematic evaluation process designed to provide evidence that will inform decisions on what to improve. The results are not generalizable; they are situational, interpreted and made meaningful by the very practitioners who make the decisions. Reminding professionals about the essence of what it is all about will allow them the freedom to explore ways to embed outcomes-based assessment in their day-to-day activities.

9

COLLABORATION

A ccording to *Merriam Webster's Online Dictionary*, the definition of *collaborate* is "1: to work jointly with others or together especially in an intellectual endeavor, 2: to cooperate with or willingly assist an enemy of one's country and especially an occupying force, 3: to cooperate with an agency or instrumentality with which one is not immediately connected" (see http://www.merriam-webster.com/dictionary/collaboration). While it may appear to be more entertaining to focus on definition number two as it relates to postsecondary organizations, this chapter will focus on the meaning behind, and the corresponding practices of, definitions one and three.

As you examine these definitions, you may find it fascinating to see that numbers one and three are listed as separate definitions of the meaning of collaborate. For example, if the focus on a project of collaboration is an intellectual endeavor, would the reader assume that a particular intellectual endeavor automatically creates a mutual connection between those working jointly? Indeed, the apparent challenge to collaboration in 2- and 4- year institutions in the United States is often because of the parties' not recognizing that their intellectual endeavors may mean they are inherently connected. Rather, we appear to have separate aspirations within the academy itself (Kezar, 2003; Schuh, 1999). In 4-year institutions, academics have aspirations of research productivity while the student affairs professionals have aspirations of student success. But does that assumption truly apply to all faculty and administrators at a 4-year institution? And what about those at 2-year institutions?

If these assumptions are not true and we are all connected by the mutual intellectual endeavor of organizing ourselves to see that students succeed, then is our challenge to implement effective collaboration brought about by the separateness of our departmental or unit organizational structures, as definition number three would imply (Kramer, 2007; Love & Estanek, 2004; Schuh, 1999)? Could it be that our position descriptions, promotion and rewards structures, and work environments do not allow us to align ourselves with the common intellectual endeavor of organizing and delivering student success (Craig, 2003)?

Common Barriers to Collaboration

There are several reported common barriers to collaboration. Oregon State University student affairs professionals describe a common barrier as the belief "that student learning belongs in the domain of the teaching faculty and does not include student affairs professionals" (Sanderson & Ketcham, 2007). This barrier was also noted by a number of good-practice institutions. Why is it that this belief or attitude may be held by members of the academic and student affairs sides of the academy? Where is the evidence that this is not simply an uneducated perspective that can easily be overcome through education or through identifying a common need that unites both sides of the academy? Regardless of the pervasiveness of this belief and regardless of its origin, when one desires to educate another to change his or her beliefs, often the motivation on the part of the one who will be educated is missing. In other words, you may want to educate another about the importance of your belief or practice, but what is the other person's motivation to learn from you? Why should the person care about what you have to say? So to eliminate the belief that student affairs professionals have no role in student learning, a desire to change the belief must be established, and the motivation for learning a new belief must be provided. The approach to resolving this barrier is discussed later in this chapter.

Another barrier not often recognized by faculty or student affairs professionals, which may be the most pertinent, is that faculty's position descriptions, rewards, and promotion processes do not reflect the desire for faculty to improve student success and/or learning (Bresciani, in press-a; Craig, 2003). People tend to spend their time according to what they value or what they are told to value (Bresciani, 2006; Love & Estanek, 2004). Therefore, if faculty are hired and evaluated for the extent to which they deliver courses and/or research publications rather than the extent to which they contribute collaboratively to designing curriculum and support programs that enhance student success, it is obvious where faculty will invest their time. Faculty, particularly nontenured faculty, will invest their time in what they are told to value. So, while some faculty may see themselves aligned with student affairs professionals in the common intellectual endeavor of designing curricula, support programs, and out-of-classroom applications of learning (e.g., the cocurricular), they are not rewarded for these collaborative activities, and in some cases their participation in this work may become detrimental to their ability to keep their position. They literally may lose the respect of their colleagues who perceive them as focusing too much time on student learning and development and not enough time on research.

Administrators at Alverno College took a unique approach to collaboration involving student learning. Staff from various departments in academic and student affairs met to discuss the overall educational process at Alverno. Eventually, the group

> produced a paper entitled, *Partners in Learning: Staff Collaboration in Promoting Student Learning Across the College*. This paper is introduced to and discussed with all new employees during their orientation to the College. The concepts represented in this paper introduce the faculty and staff to the importance of their role in providing a positive learning environment and assisting students to be successful. (Bresciani et al., 2009)

However, oftentimes there are still barriers to be faced in collaboration. If we return for just a moment to the three definitions of collaboration, the barrier created by faculty being rewarded for things other than student success means that we are considering collaboration in the context of definition number three. This means that while many faculty do, in fact, see themselves united with student affairs professionals toward a common intellectual endeavor of student success, the structures they work in are very separate (Banta & Kuh, 1998; Kramer, 2007; Kuh & Banta, 2000; Schuh, 1999). Faculty rewards and, often, hiring structures do not allow faculty to be united with student affairs professionals toward the common goal of student success. Thus, we must approach student and academic affairs collaborations with this in mind. We must no longer assume that faculty do not believe that student affairs professionals can contribute to discussions of improving student learning; rather, we must strive to design collaborations that are sustainable given the differing structures and reward systems.

Issues to Address Before Developing Collaborations

As you hear student affairs professionals express concerns about collaborations with faculty, you will often hear a great deal of blame being placed on faculty for the failed collaboration. These remarks resemble the concerns stated previously, such as student affairs professionals' not being welcomed into conversations of student learning or that faculty do not have time for or care about student learning. You may also find yourself listening to comments about varying expectations of student learning, diverging conceptual frameworks, and differing ideas about delivering learning (Bresciani et al., in press). Often, you will be told that there were personality conflicts or that the attitudes of those involved were just not quite "right." Kezar (2003) points out that student affairs professionals were very successful in designing and implementing collaborative projects with faculty because of their engaging personalities and their ability to demonstrate cooperative skills and positive attitudes and to articulate common goals.

Based on Kezar's (2003) study, we may find it beneficial to address a few items prior to engaging faculty in collaborative exercises. For example, we may find it helpful to not assume that student affairs professionals have cooperation skills. We may want to provide them with opportunities to learn those skills as well as other skills that promote collaboration (Bresciani, in press-c). If we can provide student affairs professionals with effective skill sets for collaboration, it may mean that these professionals can counterbalance personalities that tend not to engage or be collaborative.

While attitude and personality are difficult to influence, education among student affairs professionals on why faculty may be less predisposed to collaborative behavior would most assuredly assist with any collaborative effort (Barr, 2000; Love & Estanek, 2004; Schuh, 1999). As discussed earlier, hiring, rewards, and promotion of faculty do not reflect the criteria that student affairs professionals often try to promote in their work. Thus, helping student affairs professionals understand this fact may create a shift in attitude from blame to understanding (Craig, 2003). And with understanding, creativity can flow to assist in proposing very real solutions needed to create collaborative relationships and programs.

Attitudes and understanding of common goals can commence from a place of shared knowledge if student affairs professionals are well versed on learning and development theories and their applications (Love & Estanek,

2004). Sometimes student affairs professionals are not necessarily well versed in student development and learning theories, or they may not fully communicate the theories that undergird their work (Bresciani, in press-c). Therefore, when faculty view the work of student affairs professionals, they only see activity that is void of the theories that form the foundation of the practice. Articulating the theories that are in practice may begin to open doors of collaboration where faculty recognize the linkage of the student affairs professionals' work to the work that faculty do and value (Bloland, Stamatakos, & Rogers, 1996).

Thus, as this book illustrates, it is imperative when approaching faculty to invite engagement in collaborative efforts that student affairs professionals fully understand the theories that inform their practice, that they articulate the outcomes for their practice, and that they design assessment plans to inform the improvement of the programs they design (Banta & Kuh, 1998; Bresciani, in press-c; Kuh & Banta, 2000; Love & Estanek, 2004; Schuh, 1999). Furthermore, the more student affairs professionals can learn about what a faculty member intends for the student to learn, the more they can incorporate those outcomes into their own work (Banta & Kuh, 1998; Haessig & La Potin, 2004). This will set the stage for collaborations that honor what faculty have already articulated, what faculty expect their students to learn.

Finally, and maybe the most difficult challenge, is to learn to manage one's own ego, which often comes into play when learning cooperation and collaboration skills. However, ego management is also important when ideas are created and, most importantly, when they are implemented. First, it is not easy to go to others and ask for their ideas, needs, and thoughts when you already know what the solution or plan should be. It is also not easy on anyone to be in a room, asking just the right questions at just the right time, waiting for those in the room to formulate the ideas or implementation plans for the project that you drafted months ago. However, it is important to do so if you want the project to thrive and if you want faculty genuinely engaged.

One thing we know about many academic cultures is that ownership and deliberation of ideas is very important (Bolman & Deal, 1991; Kezar, 2001; Schuh, 1999). Many times as administrators we do not feel we have the patience or time for deliberation. We hurry past the value of the free and frank discourse that many faculty have come to know and expect. For some personalities, these conversations are nothing short of painful. Sometimes these conversations can even feel demeaning as our expressed ideas seem to fall on deaf ears only to be spoken moments later verbatim by someone else and adopted enthusiastically by all. For other personalities, this process is exhilarating. Regardless of your affinity, the process is important in higher education and must be followed if the collaboration is to be sustained beyond individual personalities and informal relationships.

Steps to Establishing Sustainable Collaborations

Given all this information, where would one start if one was interested in forming collaborations or strengthening those already in existence? There are many resources and much guidance for forming collaborations. The following steps synthesize much of what is in the literature (Banta & Kuh, 1998; Haessig & La Potin, 2004; Kezar, 2003; Kramer, 2007; Kuh & Banta, 2000; Love & Estanek, 2004; Manning et al., 2006) and include ideas gleaned from professionals engaged in collaborative practice.

1. Provide student affairs professionals with professional development in (a) cooperation and collaboration skills, (b) how to apply the learning and development theories that undergird their work, and (c) how to assess the intended learning and development outcomes.

   As discussed previously, the provision of professional development demonstrates a commitment of leadership to the values of the organization (Banta & Kuh, 1998; Kezar, 2003). At Isothermal Community College, the administration allocates resources to have part-time staff cover offices within the division on a regular basis:

   > Having staff in place to cover offices has enabled the entire, full-time staff to meet on a regular (typically monthly) basis in order to engage in assessment tasks and training. We believe that this broad based participation among all staff including professionals and those in support roles has proven essential in making assessment part of the fabric of departmental life and cultivating buy-in for assessment in student services. (Bresciani et al., in press)

   If the leadership of an organization is committed to engaging in collaborative practices, in programming for and supporting student learning and development, and in assessing the effectiveness of its practice, the leadership will be committed to providing time for these professional development opportunities such as those at Isothermal Community College. This is especially true if the organization has not yet had time to seek collaborative skills, knowledge of student learning and development theories and their application, and assessment in the organization's hiring structures. This leads to the next step.

2. Review hiring practices and performance evaluations to determine whether collaboration is indeed a part of the hiring criteria and used as a component in performance reviews, promotions, and rewards (Bresciani, in press-a; Kezar, 2003; Love & Estanek, 2004). Similar to faculty, if student affairs professionals are not rewarded for their efforts to design, implement, and evaluate collaborative programs, we can expect that the practice will not become sustainable over time. This will only occur with those practitioners whose personalities are conducive to collaboration and who form relationships around collaboration.

3. Be sure your ego is in check. While this is an ongoing challenge throughout all steps in the process, it begins when one first approaches faculty to ask how one can be of service (Love & Estanek, 2004). The act of approaching faculty to ask how you can help does not, as it may feel, render you subservient. Rather, it is the first step in opening the door of collaboration. While many faculty may simply not know how to answer your request, your offer will likely be received with gratitude.

4. Provide the motivation for faculty to engage in collaborative projects (Craig, 2003; Haessig & La Potin, 2004; Kezar, 2003). Since many faculty may not know how to answer your request to help them, you may have to establish a need for them to ask for assistance. In other words, you may have to leverage a current need you know they have and that you know you can fully offer your assistance to address successfully.

   Leveraging the faculty's need for engaging in outcomes-based assessment or their desire to use data in their decision-making processes can drive the formation of collaborations (Aviles, 2000;

Banta & Kuh, 1998; Craig, 2003; Yeater, Miltenberger, Laden, Ellis, & O' Donohue, 2001). To do this, you will need to do your homework. This may require you to learn about the professional accreditation processes of some programs or simply learn the outcomes of general education or the institutional learning principles. In addition, you may want to become familiar with the regional accreditation requirements so that you can speak clearly about how you can specifically help faculty design and assess learning and development in the curricular and cocurricular. Furthermore, if you can demonstrate how the collaborative work may result in one or more publications (which will require you to learn about those possibilities), you will further demonstrate your understanding of faculty needs, and your offer of assistance will be even more greatly appreciated.

5. Develop collective goals rather than presenting your goals to faculty (Banta & Kuh, 1998; Colwell, 2006; Haessig & La Potin, 2004; Hirsch & Burack, 2001; Kezar, 2003; Schuh, 1999). Sometimes, when student affairs professionals approach faculty with the request to collaborate, they tell faculty what they need from them rather than offering assistance to meet faculty goals. Again, managing the ego in this approach is important as we realize that faculty are often fully consumed by their workload. In any event, while faculty may understand our needs and want to help, they simply, as previously mentioned, cannot afford to risk the well-being of their own positions.

Therefore, if we can learn what faculty value about student learning and development and then approach aligning our goals to faculty values and goals, we will be farther down the road in our collaborative project. This conversation does take time, and again, the collaboration may dissolve before it begins as student affairs professionals become frustrated with the lack of time faculty members can contribute to these conversations. So the more student affairs professionals can request documents such as general education outcomes and assessment plans, expected college learning outcomes, professional accreditation requirements, regional accreditation requirements, and course syllabi, the more they can envision how the collaboration will work and the more they can align their own programs and values with the needs and values of faculty members.

As these conversations progress, the barriers of beliefs and assumptions will melt away as student affairs professionals lead the discussion that clarifies differences in perspectives and conceptual frameworks for delivery of learning and its assessment (Kezar, 2003; Love & Estanek, 2004; Manning et al., 2006). These conversations also allow faculty and student affairs professionals to plan the curriculum and cocurriculum together as they plan its assessment (Banta & Kuh, 1998; Manning et al., 2004; Schuh, 1999). Doing so contributes to a more sustainable, long-term collaborative effort.

For example, at Alverno College, the administration carved out community time for everyone to work together to promote student learning. Some examples include

- common workshops for faculty and student affairs professionals;
- a weekly meeting of faculty and student affairs professionals to review the issues first-year students face; and
- common free time for meetings and events from noon to 1 p.m. daily (Bresciani et al., in press).

Although these suggestions may not be feasible at every institution, one or more may be modified and/or implemented. An occasional workshop or meeting would allow conversations to occur while not requiring an initial long-term commitment.

As these conversations move forward, remember to practice patience during the deliberation process (Kezar, 2003; Pace, Blumreich, & Merkle, 2006). Do not underestimate the value of piloting the project while faculty deliberate. Piloting the project in small ways allows you to collect evidence of its effectiveness. The evidence will allow you to demonstrate the value of the project as you gather helpful information on how to improve the project.

6. Commit the time to do the work successfully. While this most likely goes without saying, collaborations often fall apart because people approach them with the mentality that shared work takes less time. Those of us who have engaged in collaborative projects with faculty recognize that while the work is strengthened and enriched by the collaboration, it sometimes feels as if we are doing all the work. Thus, before agreeing to enter into a collaborative project, make sure you

have scheduled the time not only to gather the information discussed previously so that shared goals can be established but to plan, implement, and assess the work intended (Banta & Kuh, 1998).

Finally, if the environment and the culture are suitable, assess the collaboration. Evaluating the collaboration provides others with meaningful information about how to design and operationalize successful collaborations. Furthermore, the information gained may be used to improve the existing collaboration.

7. Build formal structures that reward and support collaboration that will continue beyond personalities and informal relationships (Kezar, 2003). Many collaborations are based on personalities and relationships (Kezar). Identifying ways to systematize collaborative efforts within organizational frameworks and policies will promote sustainability beyond the people involved. For example, at Colorado State University, "maintaining both academic and student affairs assessment plans in the same University database symbolizes the emphasis the University places on collaboration between student affairs and academic programs to affect student learning and character development" (Bresciani et al., 2009).

Examples of Successful Collaborations

Examples of successful collaboration vary greatly in size and scale. At Frederick Community College,

> the vice president created the "First Wednesday" meeting time—a time in which managers are freed to caucus staff and faculty across the organization to discuss issues of mutual concern, examine business processes, and explore the feasibility of new services and programs. This has resulted in improved processes, program and service revisions and enhancements, and better communication within and outside the division. (Bresciani et al., in press)

At Texas A&M University,

> Student Life Studies collaborates with individual faculty members and with academic administrators on various assessment and research projects. Some departments provide opportunities for internships and assistantships for the academic community. Others provide direct services to students from

faculty referrals to the Student Counseling Service's Academic and Career Services programs, the Student Health Center, or the Office of the Dean of Student Life. Some of these initiatives and collaborations involve shared assessment activities. Many do not. (Bresciani et al., 2009)

The residence life department at Northern Arizona University sought out a faculty member who would be particularly interested in its assessment project based on the faculty member's background.

> The Director of Residence Life asked faculty to evaluate the physical environments of the residence halls to get a different perspective. A faculty member in the College of Business with background on marketing research, forecasting, and consumer behavior collaborated with the Director of Residence Life. The Director was doing research on what type of amenities and features students would like in an apartment-style residence hall. The faculty member was able to assist in the director's research due to his experience.

The university has a great amount of collaboration with student affairs professionals, faculty, students, and administrators in its annual Assessment Fair, which displays assessment projects and research from individuals involved in many facets of the university (Bresciani et al., in press).

Oregon State University has an extensive collaboration effort between "the Colleges of Business and Engineering and the University Housing and Dining Services with regard to a living and learning community entitled the Austin Entrepreneurship Program" (Sanderson & Ketcham, 2007).

> The Austin Entrepreneurship Program at Weatherford Residential College is a unique living-learning environment for undergraduates offering entrepreneurship courses, hands-on experience, and the opportunity to explore business ideas. The Weatherford program focuses on four key initiatives: (1) entrepreneurship and innovation, (2) social entrepreneurship, (3) responsible, sustainable business practice, and (4) professional development. (Oregon State University, 2007)

These four examples illustrate successful collaboration efforts between students and academic affairs. Collaborative efforts can range from inviting a faculty member to speak at a student affairs program to developing institution-wide learning outcomes. The important thing is to take steps toward collaboration whenever possible to create a seamless learning environment for each student who attends your institution (Schuh, 1999).

FUNDING AND OTHER RESOURCES

As with almost any project, program, or initiative on college and university campuses today, resources are an important issue, particularly when it comes to outcomes-based assessment. The literature suggests that a lack of resources is one of the primary obstacles faced by those engaging in any assessment process (Bresciani, 2006; Palomba & Banta, 1999; Schuh et al., 2001; Upcraft & Schuh, 1996). According to Upcraft and Schuh, it is important to recognize that the assessment process should be supported with at least a minimal level of resources before beginning any project. Limited funding, time, and human resources are all potential challenges during an outcomes-based assessment process. Each of these challenges will be examined in greater detail in the following sections.

Funding

It is unlikely that outcomes-based assessment can be effectively completed without funding. The amount of funding necessary varies extensively depending on the existence of centralized institutional resources and the scope of the project at hand. Assessment is rarely free, but it does not have to break the bank in order to be done well. Schuh et al. (2001) agree that assessment does not have to be expensive. According to the authors, reallocation of time, collaboration, and use of on-campus experts for various tasks (e.g., data analysis) can keep the costs of assessment within a reasonable limit (Bresciani, 2006; Schuh et al.). Collaborating with faculty members well versed in data analysis will lower the costs of using outside experts. More-over, reallocating the time of student affairs administrators and other profes-sionals who can help document the process, communicate the results, and find innovative ways of doing the work for less will contribute to lower costs for outcomes-based assessment.

It is important to consider all aspects of the assessment process when determining the amount of funding necessary to complete a particular proj-ect. More often than not, those engaged in assessment planning fail to take into account the costs associated with the evaluation piece when budgeting and financing the project. Evaluation, according to Upcraft and Schuh (1996), involves using the results of assessment for improvement at any level of an organization. This common oversight may be because many see the assessment cycle ending with the communication of results. They often do not take their planning to the next step to consider the potential costs associ-ated with the changes that may result from the information obtained from the findings. Thus, it is important to ponder the implications of evaluation and to set some funding aside. If this is not an option, it is imperative to at least consider the means available to secure funding or the manner in which funding reallocations will be made to finance needed change resulting from assessment findings.

When determining costs associated with assessment, questions similar to the ones that follow should be asked:

1. What types of instruments or methodologies will be used to collect the data?
2. How will the data be analyzed and by whom?
3. What types of technology and technological support will be used?
4. Who will be involved in the assessment process and in what ways?
5. How will the results of the assessment be communicated?
6. What kind of professional development is needed to implement the planned assessment methods, data analysis, interpretation of the data, and communication of the findings?

These questions, though seemingly simple in nature, will enable those in charge of the assessment process to get a more accurate view of all of the potential costs.

Once these questions are answered, the anticipated monetary costs of an assessment project can be determined, and compromises or changes can be made. In addition to allocating departmental, divisional, and institutional finances for assessment purposes, external grants and funding opportunities should be sought (Bresciani, 2006). At Texas A&M, "the Division of Student Affairs [was] the beneficiary of some funding based on the University's Quality Enhancement Plan" (Bresciani et al., 2009).

Funding to help support the costs of supplies, analysis, or other parts of the process may be obtained through partnering with external groups, such as national professional organizations or government grant agencies that are interested in particular aspects of student learning (e.g., leadership development of women or the development of an ethic of care among students at a Jesuit college). Working with the office associated with development on campus to secure alumni or other donations specifically targeted to assist with the assessment of student learning is a unique way of acquiring funds. Finally, increasing numbers of divisions of student affairs are creating development offices specifically focused on raising money for student affairs work. Part of these funds can be earmarked for assessment of student learning and may be used to offset the costs incurred. Finally, it may be helpful to realize the effectiveness of using outcomes-based assessment data for internal reallocation of funds, as well as seeking additional funds for projects.

Whenever planning new projects, it is important for proposals to include the costs of assessing their effectiveness. If an assessment budget line for every project can be considered standard protocol, then student affairs organizations will no longer continue to consider assessment as an added expense but rather simply a part of the cost of doing their day-to-day business.

Time

A second resource that is important when engaging in outcomes-based assessment is time, which is a hot commodity on college and university campuses. The perception of the availability of time will enhance or detract from a successful assessment process. Time for assessment not only includes time to collect and analyze data. It also includes time to educate members of the student affairs division and the university community about assessment as well as its merit for identifying and enhancing student learning (Bresciani, 2006). Time should be allotted to develop assessment plans, implement those plans, and reflect upon those plans, as well as document what has occurred during the assessment process and disseminate and use the findings (Bresciani, 2006). Those involved may need time to learn how to do all these steps in addition to the time it will take to actually do them. Finally, time to plan, develop, and implement the changes that result from the assessment is also needed. As one can see, time is the resource that is the greatest priority when implementing the assessment process.

Because time is a valuable resource, those spearheading the assessment process must work with campus leaders to make assessment a priority, insisting that some time be specifically set aside for the outcomes-based assessment process. Just as monies can be redistributed to cover the costs of the process, time can be reordered to ensure that manageable and meaningful assessment can occur. A visible commitment to outcomes-based assessment in student affairs is necessary on the part of institutional, divisional, and departmental leaders. Connecting outcomes-based assessment to organizational priorities such as strategic planning, budgeting, and continuous improvement processes demonstrates its significance and makes it a part of routine daily activities. At Paradise Valley Community College, "ultimately assessment came to be viewed and accepted by staff as a 'normal' part of the existing organizational systems and an essential everyday lens to view the delivery of programs and services" (Bresciani et al., 2009). This is the ideal practice: for outcomes-based assessment to become a part of normal day-to-day operations.

Furthermore, when assessment is an institutional, divisional, and/or departmental priority, policies can be made and practices implemented to ensure that ample time is allocated for this task. Peterson and Augustine (2000) assert, "The extent to which institutions develop specific management policies and practices is linked to the level of support for student assessment within the institution" (p. 25). Student affairs professionals may understand and support the need for assessment but may already feel as if their plates were full in terms of responsibilities. They may, however, make assessment a more integral part of their work if there are policies in place that assist with the prioritization of time. At Isothermal Community College,

> the first priority in engaging busy student services staff in assessment efforts is setting aside time for assessment. At ICC this would not be possible

without the support of the administration that allots resources on an ongoing basis to support part-time staff persons in covering the office. (Bresciani et al., 2009)

Making assessment a priority in departmental, divisional, or institutional strategic plans will establish it as an issue of importance for the organization. Placing assessment at the forefront of an institutional document will demonstrate its significance in the eyes of key leaders and, therefore, the organization. It will also lend support to student affairs professionals as they reorganize their time, resources, and efforts to undertake the assessment process. As stated earlier, including funding of assessment in project planning and annual action planning illustrates the value of evidence-based decision making. Additionally, demonstrating that assessment findings inform annual budgeting decisions will, once again, demonstrate its significance in the institutional fabric. Likewise, department heads will be required to have priority conversations about how resources are allocated to improving student success, therefore making assessment a more integral part of their daily and yearly work.

Human Resources

In addition to time and money, people who are willing and able to carry out assessment are the third major resource necessary for effective assessment. In chapter 5, we discuss the various parties that should be included in disseminating and using the results of an outcomes-based assessment process. Those groups include senior institutional leaders (e.g., presidents, vice presidents, deans, and directors), boards of trustees, department heads, faculty, administrators, student affairs practitioners, and students. Each of these stakeholders may also serve as a resource for the assessment process.

By making assessment an institutional priority, boards of trustees and senior leaders demonstrate their significance within an organization. Simple gestures, such as asking about assessment of student learning, results, and evaluation, will take little time and energy but will clearly demonstrate that outcomes-based assessment of student learning should be occurring. As mentioned previously, incorporating assessment into mission statements, strategic plans, and primary institutional documents makes a public statement about the value placed on assessment of student learning within an organization. Additionally, incorporating assessment skills and knowledge into job descriptions and hiring individuals with assessment expertise and experience will further support the development of a culture of assessment in an organization (see chapter 9, pp. 152–156, for specific suggestions for this approach).

Division and department leaders may then feel comfortable redefining their roles and the roles of those administrators and practitioners who report to them to make assessment a part of their work. Assessment is considered to be a daunting task by many. Therefore, incorporating it into current practice, as opposed to making it a task in and of itself, may help alleviate some of the almost immediate avoidance and fear that often accompanies it. Additionally, tapping into those individuals in divisions and departments who seem to have a knack for and interest in assessment will help lessen the dissent for many. Redefining their job descriptions to include assessment of student learning will provide the twofold benefit of giving them an opportunity to broaden their professional experiences while allowing them to attend to assessment needs. This will allow those who are not directly involved in student assessment to take on other responsibilities that may showcase their own talents and interests.

Forming committees such as an assessment committee or a learning outcomes committee can be of vital importance in the assessment process. These committees can develop timelines for the assessment process and help in the evaluation of the overall process, and they are also a valuable resource for other members of the division to consult with during every step of the outcomes-based assessment process. At Oregon State University, "an Assessment Council comprised of volunteers from many different departments in student affairs began the work of educating themselves and then educating others about assessment" (Bresciani et al., 2009). "The associate dean coordinated assessment related activities at Widener University. In consultation with the assistant provost for student learning assessment, the associate dean coordinated activities aimed at engaging staff, gathering input and assessment data, and providing feedback" (Bresciani et al., 2009).

Finally, as stated repeatedly throughout this book, collaborating with people throughout the university will provide ample resources for assessment. Many faculty members are skilled in research methods and are often willing to assist with creating instruments and data analysis. Others may be willing to lend expertise throughout the process by sitting on committees or acting as consultants. Exploring the myriad of on-campus human resources available for use in assessment may result in increased savings in time and money.

Additional Resources

Time, money, and human capital are the three primary resources for effective outcomes-based assessment. Bresciani (2006) highlighted a number of additional resources that may augment the assessment process in student affairs, some of which are elaborated on further in chapter 11. Preexisting institutional research and survey data may be of great use to student affairs professionals engaging in outcomes-based assessment. Using data that are collected at the institutional level but analyzed with indicators specific to the cocurricular experience will save the time, money, and human resources that are generally expended on the creation of instruments and data collection. Moreover, using online Web resources, templates, survey development tools, and documentation tools (Bresciani, 2006) will assist in the development of an effective assessment process and will avoid wasting time and other coveted resources on reinventing the wheel for outcomes-based assessment. Talk with professional colleagues, engage in Web-based research, and investigate current assessment literature to get ideas and find tips for engaging in efficient outcomes-based assessment. Establishing what has worked for others may save countless hours and energy that can be expended on other pressing issues and responsibilities.

Additionally, Bresciani (2006) suggests using consultants, engaging faculty or administrative fellows, and providing professional development to enhance assessment knowledge and skills. All serve as a means of educating people about outcomes-based assessment in affordable ways. Consultants can range from national experts to institutional faculty to student affairs professionals at benchmarked institutions who have successfully engaged in assessment of student learning. The type of consultant employed is contingent upon the scope of the consultation needed, the funding available to reimburse the consultant for travel and consultation fees, and the timeline at hand.

Faculty or administrative fellows who are knowledgeable about outcomes-based assessment may also provide insight and assistance where needed (Bresciani, 2006). Fellowships are a means of collaborating with faculty on one's own campus or from other institutions of higher education interested in researching and practicing assessment to solve the sometimes complex assessment puzzle. Likewise, administrative fellowships provide opportunities to partner with professionals who are very knowledgeable about outcomes-based assessment and student affairs. This can serve as a great asset to any effective assessment process. Similar to consultants, fellowships may be expensive and costs should be considered when determining whether this resource is a good fit for one's institution.

Professional development is an additional means of educating student affairs administrators who may be interested in learning more about assessment in general (Bresciani, 2006). A number of regional and national assessment-specific conferences are held each year, and many professional organizations now include an assessment component in their curriculum. Additionally, many Web-based conferences and educational sessions are available for this purpose. Again, time, funding, and scope of knowledge needed should be taken into account when determining which type of professional development is best for one's institution.

Finally, creative human resource management may assist in the realization of assessment goals. Bresciani (2006) suggests release time as a means of resource reallocation for outcomes-based assessment. Releasing student affairs professionals from their traditional responsibilities to attend specifically to assessment needs provides a concrete period of time to specifically focus on assessment without the additional stress of other work-related items. Time specifically focused on assessment may increase creativity and enhance the quality of the end product. In addition to a potentially more creative and better assessment product, the reallocation of time and responsibility may reduce costs by eliminating the need to hire additional assessment experts or help during the assessment planning process.

Of significant importance is simply this: The discovery of how well our services and programs are working via outcomes-based assessment means that we can make better decisions about where to improve effectiveness and efficiency. Having discussions informed by assessment findings about what can be improved and how means that through this process we are increasing quality and having discussions about how much quality can be increased. Without the evidence generated from assessment, the conversations about what to do on a day-to-day basis are at risk of being influenced by factors that may have little to do with the quality of student success. Ask yourself if your organization can really afford not to implement such a process.

11

RESOURCES AND RECOMMENDATIONS FOR FUTURE PRACTICE

While this book contains references to resources and recommendations for practice, this chapter explores these two areas in more depth. First, we discuss resources to be used in the support of assessment of student learning and development. Second, we include a discussion of future directions to consider in the implementation of assessment of student learning and development in student affairs.

General Resources

General resources to support assessment include texts/reading lists, Web sites, discussion groups, conferences and workshops, students/faculty/other professionals, consultants, and technological tools to assist student affairs practitioners in their continued learning and development of outcomes-based assessment. The following resources were compiled at the time of this book's printing. We encourage the readers to explore the Web sites provided to continue to update their own list of resources. Appendix A is a list of other suggested readings.

Web Sites

The Web site that contains the most comprehensive list of assessment resources is maintained by Ephraim Schechter and is housed at North Carolina State University at http://www2.acs.ncsu.edu/UPA/assmt/resource.htm. These materials undergo a quality control evaluation, as Schechter examines everything posted to this site. The Web site is comprehensive and incredibly helpful, yet it is not always easy to navigate for those newest to assessment. At first it may seem quite lengthy, as all the material is on one page; however, the search feature works very well. In this chapter, we unpacked a bit of the information contained on this site to make it easier for readers to find.

Discussion Listservs

The online discussion lists in this section were extracted from http:// www2.acs.ncsu.edu/UPA/assmt/resource.htm. In addition, NASPA (www .naspa.org) and the ACPA (http://www.myacpa.org/) have assessment groups in their organizations that have their own blogs, workshops, conferences, and other networking and resource materials.

Other discussion boards that are not specific to student affairs but include very helpful conversations include

- ASSESS: includes a wide range of topics relevant to assessment in higher education. To subscribe, visit http://www.uky.edu/Education/ EDP/assesslist.html
- COMFO (College Outcomes Measurement Forum Online): includes an interdisciplinary look at assessment in higher education. Subscribe at http://www.collegeoutcomes.com/lvi/COMFO.htm
- EVALTALK: discusses topics involving evaluation. Many topics include conversations on outcomes-based assessment. For subscribing information, visit http://mirror.undp.org/niger/pnudfr/rense/Forum uk.html
- FYA-List: devoted to topics involving assessment during students' freshman year. To subscribe, visit http://www.sc.edu/fye/listservs/ subscrib.html
- ICSSIA: hosts the Practical Assessment Community of Practice. To join, visit http://icssia.org/communities/index.cfm
- ASSESS-W: specifically looks at assessing writing. Information on subscribing is available at http://www.lsoft.com/SCRIPTS/WL.EX E?SLi=ASSESS-W&H=LISTSERV.LOUISVILLE.EDU

For more assessment-related discussion lists including portfolios and retention, visit Assessment in Higher Education's Web site at http://ahe .cqu.edu.au/discussion_lists.htm

Conferences and Workshops

A great way to build networks of people to call on for help and to further your and your team's professional development is to attend conferences and workshops. Given the increasing focus on accountability, outcomes-based assessment conferences and workshops are springing up across the country. We encourage you to seek out the expertise that locally developed conferences and workshops can lend, and we further encourage you to consider hosting your own campus conference or workshop, which is a wonderful opportunity to learn what others are doing on your campus and to showcase your own institution's fine work. If you consider hosting your own conference, remember to include all aspects of your campus life (e.g., academics, business and finance, student affairs, facilities). Doing so creates opportunities for exchanges and adaptation of ideas as well as opportunities to connect values and determine the many ways that cross-functional areas are contributing to the improvement of student learning and development. These kinds of events reinforce the fact that everyone has a role in supporting student success.

Lists of national and regional assessment conferences and workshops are maintained by

- Assessment Conferences (ACAT): http://www.assessmentconferences .com/
- Illinois State University: http://www.assessment.ilstu.edu/workshops/
- University of Minnesota: http://www.academic.umn.edu/provost/ teaching/cesl_national.html
- University of Nebraska at Kearney: http://www.unk.edu/academic affairs/assessment/Resources/index.php?id=4437
- University of Northern Iowa: http://www.uni.edu/assessment/con ferences.shtml

A list of international assessment conferences can be found at http:// www.chea.org/intdb/QA-organizations.asp

Students and Faculty

While many campuses use skilled consultants to move their work forward, we encourage you to include the talented professionals you may have already on your campus or in your community. As we have illustrated in previous chapters, there are several ways to incorporate the gifts and skills of students, faculty, and each other in the assessment process, allowing the process to become sustainable. Again, you are attempting to build habits of self-reflection into each day rather than creating processes and projects that require large amounts of money and time. Some reminders and suggestions for involving students in this process include the following:

1. Ask students to write outcomes for any activities they are requesting you to provide. Doing so will move them from the habit of simply providing activities to reflecting on what they want to have accomplished as an end result.

2. Invite students to comment on outcomes you wrote, methods of delivering those outcomes, and the means and criteria for evaluating those outcomes. Doing so will help you clarify criteria and intended end results. Clarity of what you expect from students will empower students to connect your expectations with the way they make meaning and will allow them to take more responsibility for their learning and development.

3. Consider the wisdom in beginning the assessment of student learning and development in your office by first evaluating the learning and development of the paraprofessionals in your office. If the paraprofessionals understand clearly how, why, and what you want their peers to understand, they will be able to help you evaluate larger audiences.

4. Be sure to include students as you report the findings of your evaluation methods. As you do so, listen to their interpretation and ideas for improvements. Incorporate the ideas when you are able to do so.

5. Be sure to report to students the decisions and recommendations that were made from the assessment process. This creates continued ownership in the process, and they will be able to see how their ideas were used.

Faculty

Reminders for involving faculty in this process are the same as those for involving students. In addition, we encourage you to reconsider the ideas presented in chapters 6, 9, and 10.

Each Other

Many of the ways you collaborate with faculty are the ways you collaborate with each other. Understanding what each other is doing with regard to assessment is key in forming linkages of values. For example, if you understand what each other's intended outcomes are for projects, you can see where you have expressed shared values in the end results of your programs. Furthermore, you can identify ways to collaboratively deliver and evaluate those outcomes. Such collaboration provides for efficiency in time and other resource allocations.

As you link your program outcomes to divisional and institutional learning goals in your assessment plan, you can also begin to see how the day-to-day work is linking to institutional values and institutional learning outcomes. In essence, the way the institution operationalizes its values becomes clearer. For example, consider you have a program that teaches your student government leaders to prepare a well-thought-out and clearly articulated oral presentation of funding requests. You link the outcomes for these intended oral presentation skills to general education learning outcomes for oral communication and to the university learning outcomes of communication. If you make such linkages transparent, then students better understand how their cocurricular experiences align with the shared values of the institution. They literally see the alignment in your assessment plan and report with institutional values. As such, student learning is reinforced purposefully and intentionally in multiple venues across the campus. Such purposeful connections allow the student to identify the value of his or her education in a manner that can be measured, and it allows those you are connected with to assist in a collaborative design of evaluation methods and criteria as well as the analysis and interpretation of data.

As you consider leveraging the expertise of those in your institution, we encourage you to use the work of your professional associations. Many professional organizations, such as the Association of College Unions International, National Association of Student Financial Aid Administrators, National Orientation Directors Association, and other professional student affairs associations (see http://www.naspa.org), have begun to identify what students need to know and be able to do as a result of what their professionals do. For example, as career planning advisers and directors come together with other members of their professional association, they are discovering that they expect the students they work with to be able to know and perform some similar types of skills such as how to write a résumé and how to interview well. Collaborating with your professional association colleagues may mean that you are able to share commonly valued learning and development outcomes as well as the methods and criteria to evaluate them. This type of collaborative identification of outcomes assists professionals with their workloads while potentially allowing for comparison of results. We will discuss this type of comparison more later in this chapter.

Consultants

It is often necessary to invite an outside consultant to reinforce what you may have already said. It is sometimes true that an expert is not recognized as such under his or her own roof. However, we encourage you to use consultants wisely so that you do not damage the sustainability of your reflection practice. In other words, be cautious of consultants who promise a step-by-step, fill-in-the-box process. While such a process will surely accomplish the purpose, the point of engaging in outcomes-based assessment is to promote meaningful reflection and purposeful planning. A step-by-step approach doesn't always stimulate deep levels of inquiry. Issues to consider when determining whether to hire a consultant include the following:

1. Why are you bringing in the consultant? Although this may sound like a silly question, determining whether you need the consultant to do work or to train will help you decide if bringing in the consultant is building a practice you hope will become sustainable or if you are building a practice that will require continued investment in consultants.

2. If you need the consultant to do some training, consider whether sending a team to a conference may be more affordable or cost-effective than bringing in a consultant. Officials at some institutions, such as Oregon State University, have benefited greatly by sending teams to conferences. This generates new ideas among the team members, allows the team members to present their own practices at the conference and receive feedback on how to improve those practices, and provides them with additional contacts who are engaged in assessment.

3. If your student affairs professionals require some specific training that requires a consultant, consider whether negotiating for a series of training workshops that have negotiable dates may be more effective

than a one-shot training day. In this manner you are in essence purchasing professional development modules rather than an "in-and-out" consultant service. If you choose the series of training workshops, find out if you can negotiate a package fee that may cost less than individual consultancy days. In addition, ask about videotaping the training session for those not able to attend. You may also want to negotiate mass distribution and adaptation of the training materials so you can continue to use the materials in your future work. Moreover, this type of negotiation may persuade the consultant to become more invested in the success of your organization. In other words, if you purchase a progressive three-stage training module, the consultant will want to make sure the professionals are ready for the next stage, which may mean that he or she will invest more time in making sure your team is ready.

4. If you need the consultant to provide inspiration or rejuvenation for your team, be sure the consultant takes the time to learn more about the culture of your institution prior to coming, and ask if he or she can preview the work you have completed so the specifics of what you have done well can be addressed, as well as the what, why, and how of moving forward.

5. If you need the consultant to actually do some work for you, be sure to look at the details of the work needed and the required time frame. Determine whether more work will be necessary once the initial phase of the work requests is completed. In this manner, you can gauge if you are able to continue the work on your own or if more services are needed.

6. If you decide that more services will be required, consider whether negotiating a faculty member's course buyout over an academic year could provide the same services. Also consider other options such as a collaborative position hire with another local college or university or whether you can fund a graduate assistant who can be cosupervised by a faculty member or another administrator. These options may allow you to embed the work of assessment in the fabric of your institution, which will lead to sustainability. In addition, the embedding process increases ownership in what you are doing and that ultimately increases collaboration.

The following individuals and groups offer consulting, workshops, and other services to help colleges and universities plan and implement outcomes-based assessment. Please remember that this is just a list extracted from http://www2.acs.ncsu.edu/UPA/assmt/resource.htm. Therefore, it is not exhaustive and the authors do not imply a recommendation or evaluation by including this list.

- Alverno College Institute for Educational Outreach: http://www.al verno.edu/for_educators/institute.html
- Center for Education Assessment: http://www.educationassessment .org/index1_hnavbar.html
- Marilee Bresciani: http://interwork.sdsu.edu/elip/consultation/mjb _about.html
- Faculty Development Associates, Richard Lyons & Associates: http:// www.developfaculty.com/
- Hawkins Strategies Group: http://www.hawkinstrategies.com/Web pages/outcome.htm
- HigherEdAssessment.com, Ephraim Schechter: http://higheredassess ment.com/
- Insight Assessment, Peter & Noreen Facione & Associates: http:// www.insightassessment.com/consulting.html
- Institutional Effectiveness Associates, James & Karen Nichols & Associates: http://www.iea-nich.com/
- José L. Arbona (Puerto Rico): http://home.coqui.net/jarbona/arbo 541/areas/areas.html
- Kelley Assessment and Planning Services (KAPS), Larry Kelley: http://www.kelleyeducation.com/
- Mary Bold & Lillian Chenowith: http://www.boldproductions.com/
- The National Center for Higher Education Management Systems (NCHEMS): http://www.nchems.org/
- Peggy Maki Associates: http://www.peggymaki.com/
- REAP Change Consultants, Stephen Maack & Associates: http:// www.reapchange.com/
- Rockefeller Institute of Government Higher Education Program: http://www.rockinst.org/research/education/higher_education/de fault.aspx?id;eq298
- Solutions Oriented Consulting, Maggie Culp: http://maggieculp.org/

- Steve Ehrmann, director of the Flashlight program: http://www.tlt group.org/about/StephenEhrmann/ehrmann.html
- Take the Credit, Richard Laramy and Associates: http://www.utake thecredit.com/
- Virginia S. Lee & Associates: http://www.virginiaslee.com/
- Voorhees Group, Richard Voorhees & Associates: http://www.voor heesgroup.org/
- Wendy Troxel: http://people.coe.ilstu.edu/wgtroxe/consulting.htm

Technology

We, the authors, assume that if we are to meet the call for accountability and transparency, then the use of technology to demonstrate how outcomes align with institutional core values and how each unit is contributing to these outcomes is inevitable. We say this because without technology tools designed to assist those using outcomes assessment data to make decisions, it becomes more difficult to show how units are individually and collectively contributing to meeting overarching institutional learning goals. The benefit of using technology to make transparent assessment plans and reports transcends calls for accountability as well. Displaying assessment plans and reports online helps those in the division to discover what their colleagues are doing and to identify opportunities for information exchange, tool exchange, and other opportunities for collaboration. Such transparency also provides professionals with the opportunity to communicate with evidence what they are doing well.

Regardless of whether you choose to use technology to make plans and reports transparent, communicating how programmatic outcomes are aligned with institutional values becomes cumbersome without the use of technology. Consider this scenario: You are the director of assessment for a multidepartment institution. You have over 100 individual unit directors who have turned in annual assessment reports to you. You are given 2 weeks to report on how these units have improved students' writing skills. If you have over 100 paper reports, the task of completing a document analysis to determine who is actually assessing writing this year (as opposed to who assessed it last year or who has not yet assessed it at all), as well as identifying what was improved as a result, becomes overwhelming. It becomes even more overwhelming when you have only 2 weeks to complete the report.

Technological solutions, such as the open source software that Kim Bender designed at Colorado State University, allow student affairs professionals, faculty, and business and finance professionals to electronically enter their assessment plans aligning their individual unit outcomes to university learning values such as writing, speaking, critical thinking, and analytical reasoning. In addition, results from findings can be entered electronically, linking the results again to common university-wide outcomes. Decisions can be entered in the same manner. Thus, when Bender prepares a report, he can tell from the push of a few buttons who is evaluating which learning outcomes and what the person has learned from doing so. It makes the compilation of the results much more usable to higher-level decision makers who have to determine funding priorities and reallocation of resources to improve learning.

Finally, tools such as Bender's and other solutions, such as placing your assessment plans and reports on your program or institution's Web site, begin to create the transparency the public is demanding. If students can identify what you expect them to learn from participating in your student organization and you provide the data that illustrate why you expect that learning to occur from a certain level of participation in your program, you will most assuredly respond to the informational needs of these savvy consumers of learning.

Again, extracted from http://www2.acs.ncsu.edu/UPA/assmt/resource .htm, the following list of tools can be used to organize assessment plans and reports; the list of technological tools that can help you collect and analyze data or build rubrics can be found at this Web site. We do not offer this list in an attempt to endorse any particular tool but only to illustrate the types of tools that are available at the time of this book's publication. Some of these tools require the institution to invest money and a support infrastructure. Others are open source and will provide explanations of the resources that should be provided to support the systems.

- Blackboard Outcomes System is a platform for assessment processes, information, and reports, and is integrated with the Blackboard Academic Suite for course information, surveys, document and portfolio management, and user-community interaction.
- eLumen Achievement is a database for assessment processes, rubrics, results, and reports. Select How eLumen Achievement Models the Essential Process for annotated screen shots.

- CampusTools HigherEd and CampusWide from Tk20 include tools for electronic portfolios and online surveys.
- Institutional Effectiveness Associates offers guidebooks, workshops, and organizing worksheets.
- LiveText Accreditation Management System is for collecting data and organizing outcomes, rubrics, results, and so on.
- Mapping Academic Performance through e-Portfolios (myMAPP) is from the University of Nebraska at Omaha.
- Online Assessment Tracking System (OATS) and Southern Association of Colleges and Schools (SACS) Online Documentation System (SODS) are from Georgia Institute of Technology's Office of Assessment. Both programs are available for download by other institutions. An OATS user guide (pdf file) and a SODS demo are available.
- openIGOR is a free Linux-based open-source program to manage information about program outcomes and assessment-related documents; from Coker College.
- TaskStream's Accountability Management System offers competency assessment, and resource/communications management tools.
- The Teacher Education Assessment System (TEAS), the Education Program Identification Framework (EPIF), and the CEA-Candidate Tracking (CEA-CAT) from the Center for Education Assessment, facilitate National Council for Accreditation of Teacher Education (NCATE) and state-level education accreditation reviews. They can also be used to organize program assessment information in other academic areas.
- ThinkTank, from GroupSystems, facilitates collaboration and records and stores information from assessment group meetings.
- TracDat is a database for assessment processes, information, and reports; from Nuventive.
- TrueOutcomes Assessment Manager keeps track of course-level learning outcomes and can create a course outcomes matrix.
- Waypoint Outcomes keeps track of assignment-level outcomes within and across courses; from Subjective Metrics.
- WEAVEonline is a database for assessment processes, information, and reports, originally developed at Virginia Commonwealth University.

The selection of technology to assist you in the assessment process can be used to

1. Assess learning, where technology is a
   a. data collection tool or
   b. teaching tool (to promote deep learning)
2. Improve technology as a teaching tool or a data collection tool to make assessment of learning more effective
3. Improve professional development for the use of technology
4. Improve technological skills of students, faculty, student affairs professionals, and other staff
5. Improve the process of planning for improved student learning by using technology as an instructional organizational tool (Bresciani, 2008a)

It is important to be clear about the intended use of the technological tool and to be clear about how you expect to evaluate the effectiveness of the tool through outcomes-based assessment before selecting it and designing the assessment plan for the tool or for the end result of the tool.

Regardless of which technological tool you select, we provide some questions for you to consider as you use them. When considering the use of technology to promote outcomes-based assessment, consider the following:

- Does the use of this technology reinforce the reasons we are engaged in outcomes-based assessment?
- How does the use of this technology promote formative assessment, summative assessment, or the assessment of transferable skills/knowledge?
- Is our professional development to train users of our technology coupled with the professional development for outcomes-based assessment or instructional design and/or design of the delivery of the program?
- How does the use of this technology enable us to better use the results to improve student learning and development?
- How does the use of this technology improve efficiencies? And who benefits from those improved efficiencies?
- How does this technology constrain or promote creativity/flexibility within each discipline?

- How does this technology aid coordination of the process? Or does it contribute to isolated thinking and doing?
- How can data this technological tool gathers help us evaluate the extent to which we are transforming our organization through the use of evidence-based decision making?
- How does this technology help illustrate the transferability of learning/skills?
- How does this technology help us illustrate, evaluate, and improve learning/skills as they relate to the requisite skills required by employers?
- How does this technology help us determine whether the technology is promoting or prohibiting social interaction?
- How do we be certain that the technology is ensuring the deepest engagement with the subject matter?
- How will you determine that technology is promoting meaningful learning?
- What do you need to refine in all this to ensure that the technological tool serves its purpose? In other words, how do you make sure that the technological tool does not drive the practice of outcomes-based assessment but supports the practice designed by the student affairs professionals and faculty? (Bresciani, 2008a)

Considerations for Future Practice

While we do not desire to try to predict the future of outcomes-based assessment in the profession of student affairs, we do wish to reiterate some key points to consider as you move forward with the assessment of student learning and development. Many of these points are taken from Bresciani (2008b, 2008c) but are explained here with a specific application to student affairs.

First and foremost, it is important to understand that those who are demanding accountability from higher education are doing so within a framework of how they would hold a business accountable for their products. They feel that 2- and 4-year institutions should be considered as a business, and the product of that business is student learning and development (Bresciani, 2008b, 2008c). Whether or not you agree with this perspective is not the point of this chapter. We are saying that this opinion is indeed held by those who are holding us accountable and because of that, how would we organize our assessment practice to meet the demands of accountability and gather data that we can use to inform decision making?

It is our understanding that if we are held accountable for student learning and development as the product of our business, then we will be expected to compare the quality of the product, not the quality of the business that delivers the product (Bresciani, 2008b, 2008c). Thus the unit of comparison is not the institution; it is the actual learning and development. While descriptive data about the institution (i.e., business), such as biodemographic variables of 1st-year students, number of students, retention rates, number of degrees awarded in a certain time frame, may help explain why some of the outcomes of student learning and development (i.e., product) have been met or not met, those indicators are only descriptive of how the institution does its business (i.e., teaching, research, service), not how well the institution produces its product (i.e., student learning; Bresciani, 2008b, 2008c).

To discuss the quality of student learning and development (i.e., the quality of the product), we need to examine how learning and development are created or facilitated. We need to examine the quality of the people and processes that deliver the learning (i.e., design the product). That means we must examine the way the disciplines (i.e., organizational units in the business) design and deliver the learning (i.e., the product; Bresciani, 2008b, 2008c). Thus, if we want to truly understand the quality of the product (i.e., learning), we are comparing evidence of the learning of each discipline to the evidence of learning from other similar disciplines. We are not comparing the descriptive data of the organization to descriptive data of another organization. As with any organization, some disciplines (i.e., departments) are more collaborative than others. In those situations, cross-discipline conversations occur to create and deliver learning (i.e., product). Examination of quality about learning would reach across disciplines (i.e., departments).

To apply this example to student affairs, we must draw upon the notion presented earlier in this book (pp. 33–44) that each functional area of student affairs is indeed its own discipline (e.g., student leadership development, community service, student conduct, housing, financial aid, academic advising, admissions). If each functional area is a discipline, then it is complete with its own professional organization, expertise, and literature and theory that undergirds the practice of the professionals. Because of this, Bresciani (2008b, 2008c) urges student affairs professionals to consider comparing their work in their discipline with the work of others in their discipline.

To draw a comparison regionally, the professionals in the disciplines in student affairs would come to a basic agreement about student learning outcomes for their discipline. For example, representatives from career services and placement at community colleges and universities in San Diego County may come together to determine the shared outcomes of their various career preparation programs for students. The professionals would not have to implement these outcomes in the same manner; they would simply articulate shared outcomes and identify the outcomes that may vary among their institution because of varying cultures or specific descriptive characteristics of their institutions.

In this sense, this practice of articulating shared professional discipline outcomes is similar to that of other professional academic disciplines such as engineering, business, and architecture. However, in these academic disciplines, the national association's membership determines what the minimum outcomes for their profession should be. This certainly could also occur in student affairs. For example, the membership of the National Association of Colleges and Employers could convene and formulate shared student learning outcomes for students' ability to write and update their résumé, to interview effectively, or to research a career and correlating major. However, if organizations do not have these sets of outcomes in place, the discussion can start locally.

For example, if local representatives from career services meet to develop shared learning outcomes, they could benefit from the efforts of collaboratively writing these outcomes and discussing various ways to implement and evaluate them. Such conversations and exchange of ideas would most surely enrich the quality of the individual departments' outcomes-based assessment plans and reports. In addition, these professionals may also decide that comparing their results would be of value, thus creating their own professionally designed benchmarking outcomes, evaluation tools, criteria, and process.

To further illustrate, imagine that career services professionals from seven institutions within one county, representing 2- and 4-year institutions, meet to determine their common outcomes. As they discuss their outcomes, they realize that while some of the institutional professionals want to deliver the shared outcomes, they simply do not have the resources. Thus, their first step is to clearly identify which institution has learning outcomes for the profession's shared values and illustrate it in a chart (see Table 8) where yes

TABLE 8
Institutional Outcome Presence

Institution Name	Résumé Writing Present	Interview Skills Present	Career Decidedness Present	Career Exploration Present
Institution A	Yes	Yes	Yes	Yes
Institution B	No	Yes	No	Yes
Institution C	Yes	No	Yes	No
Institution D	No	No	No	No
Institution E	Yes	Yes	Yes	Yes
Institution F	Yes	Yes	Yes	Yes
Institution G	No	No	Yes	Yes

indicates that the institution does deliver learning outcomes in this area and no indicates that it does not deliver this outcome.

Using a chart such as the one in Table 8 helps students identify very quickly the institutions that have career services programs that offer what they want to gain from participation in career services. This is similar to shopping for a cell phone. If you want a cell phone that allows you to send e-mail messages, you would first see which company's cell phones offer e-mail, then you would compare the other aspects of the phone. You would not look further at a phone that didn't have a key item you needed. Similarly, if students know they will need a career services program that assists them with career exploration, they will want to know it before comparing the quality of the learning from other aspects of the program.

The next step for the local career service professionals is to determine what the learning outcomes for their shared values may be and devise a common means to evaluate those outcomes. Since they cannot agree on all their student learning and development outcomes or the way they deliver or evaluate those outcomes, they keep their conversation focused on the agreed-upon outcomes. Their institutions further identify shared ways to evaluate these outcomes, as the delivery methods are similar. For example, those who are delivering learning outcomes for résumé writing use workshops to teach students how to write résumés. They all agree on a set of criteria to evaluate the résumés. After evaluation, the professionals can take sample data from each institution and run a quick interrater reliability analysis (Bresciani, Oakleaf, Duncan, Nebeker, Barlow, Kolkhorst, & Hickmott, 2009) to determine that they have a high level of agreement. Therefore, when they compare their results, they can trust that they are indeed comparing apples to apples. If their level of agreement is not high, then they can do training to reach agreement on the rubric criteria before administering the rubric again.

The point of this illustration is that program professionals/discipline professionals can reach agreement on outcomes and the criteria for how those outcomes are evaluated. Reaching agreement allows them to compare learning within their disciplines across institutions. This is a much more meaningful comparison than simply comparing satisfaction with career services from one institution to another.

If a student examines an output similar to the presence of outcomes and their results (see Table 9), he or she is given richer data about the type of learning and development that each institution is providing in career services and how well they are providing it. In Table 9, the first four columns describe what a particular program provides, allowing the student to determine which outcomes are expected at each institution for this program. The second set of four columns represents the actual quality of learning for each outcome at each institution. This allows the student to compare the quality of learning (i.e., product) at each institution (i.e., business).

To offer further assistance in decision making, the career services professionals could determine a cost/student ratio for their service delivery and set it to a scale. Doing so would provide even more ability for decision makers to interpret the results and determine what is needed to improve. Similarly, students who desire to attend institutions with well-invested career services offices would have that information as well, even if they are only able to choose a local institution. In Table 10, the last column indicates the resource support for each student.

While these ideas may seem far-fetched, it is important to remember that transparency of student learning and development outcomes and their results is expected. If we do not choose to find a meaningful way to do this on our own as professionals in the various disciplines of student affairs, others will do it for us.

This book seeks to make the process of outcomes-based assessment meaningful and manageable. It is our intent to make the assessment process

TABLE 9

Outcome Presence and Its Results

Institution Name	Résumé Writing Present	Interview Skills Present	Career Decidedness Present	Career Exploration Present	Résumé Writing Results	Interview Skills Results	Career Decidedness Results	Career Exploration Results
				Outcome Presence and Its Results				
Institution A	Yes	Yes	Yes	Yes	Average	Good	Excellent	Excellent
Institution B	No	Yes	No	Yes	N/A	Average	N/A	Good
Institution C	Yes	No	Yes	No	Good	N/A	Good	Good
Institution D	No	No	No	No	N/A	N/A	N/A	N/A
Institution E	Yes	Yes	Yes	Yes	Excellent	Average	Poor	Good
Institution F	Yes	Yes	Yes	Yes	Good	Excellent	Excellent	Excellent
Institution G	No	No	Yes	Yes	N/A	N/A	Average	Good

TABLE 10
Outcome Presence and Its Results

Institution Name	Résumé Writing Present	Interview Skills Present	Career Decidedness Present	Career Exploration Present	Résumé Writing Results	Interview Skills Results	Career Decidedness Results	Career Exploration Results	Resource Support Level per Student
					Outcome Presence and Its Results				
Institution A	Yes	Yes	Yes	Yes	Average	Good	Excellent	Excellent	High
Institution B	No	Yes	No	Yes	N/A	Average	N/A	Good	Low
Institution C	Yes	No	Yes	No	Good	N/A	Good	Good	Medium
Institution D	No	No	No	No	N/A	N/A	N/A	N/A	Low
Institution E	Yes	Yes	Yes	Yes	Excellent	Average	Poor	Good	Low
Institution F	Yes	Yes	Yes	Yes	Good	Excellent	Excellent	Excellent	High
Institution G	No	No	Yes	Yes	N/A	N/A	Average	Good	Low

seem doable and to instill the realization that day-to-day reflection is necessary to demonstrate true accountability for shaping the lives of the next generation. While we do not want to leave the reader feeling intimidated in any way, we do want to challenge you to find ways to systematically demonstrate your contribution to student learning and development and then to move one step beyond that: embracing the notions of transparency and comparison in a manner that will further enrich the lives of students and the professional lives of those who serve them and support them in their learning and development.

APPENDIX A

SUGGESTED RESOURCES

Allen, M., & Noel, E. (2002). *Outcomes assessment handbook.* Bakersfield: California State University.

American College Personnel Association, ACUHO-I, ACUI, NACADA, NACA, NASPA, & NIRSA. (2006). *Learning reconsidered 2: Implementing a campus-wide focus on the student experience.* Washington, DC: American College Personnel Association and NASPA.

Anderson, L. W., & Krathwohl, D. R. (Eds.). (2001). *Taxonomy for learning, teaching, and assessing: A revision of Bloom's taxonomy of educational objectives.* Needham Heights, MA: Allyn & Bacon.

Anderson, M. S. (2001). The complex relations between the academy and industry: Views from the literature. *The Journal of Higher Education, 72*(2), 226–246.

Angelo, T., & Cross, P. (1993). *Classroom assessment techniques: A handbook for college teachers.* San Francisco: Jossey-Bass.

Astin, A. W. (1996). Involvement in learning revisited: Lessons we have learned. *Journal of College Student Development, 37*(2), 123–133.

Astin, A. W., & Lee, J. J. (2003). How risky are one-shot cross-sectional assessments of undergraduate students? *Research in Higher Education, 44*(6), 657–672.

Banta, T., Lund, J., Black, K., & Oblander, F. (1996). *Assessment in practice: Putting principles to work on college campuses.* San Francisco: Jossey-Bass.

Bass, B. M. (1990). *Bass and Slodgehill's handbook of leaders.* New York: The Free Press.

Bass, B. M., & Avolio, B. J. (1994). *Improving organizational effectiveness through transformational learning.* Thousand Oaks, CA: Sage.

Bennis, W. (1989). *Why leaders can't lead: The unconscious conspiracy continues.* San Francisco: Jossey-Bass.

Blimling, G. S., & Whitt, E. J. (1999). *Good practice in student affairs: Principles to foster student learning.* San Francisco: Jossey-Bass.

Bloom, B., Englehart, M., Furst, E., Hill, W., & Krathwohl, D. (1956). *Taxonomy of educational objectives: Handbook I, cognitive domain.* New York: David McKay.

Bogdan, R. C., & Biklen, S. K. (1992). *Qualitative research for education.* New York: Allyn & Bacon.

Boyer, E. (1990). *Scholarship reconsidered: Priorities of the professoriate.* Princeton, NJ: Carnegie Foundation for the Advancement of Teaching.

Brown, S. C., Stevens, R. A., Troiano, P. F., & Schneider, M. K. (2002). Exploring complex phenomena: Grounded theory in student affairs research. *Journal of College Student Development, 43*(2), 1–11.

Carr, D. (2006). Professional and personal values and virtues in education and teaching. *Oxford Review of Education, 32*(2), 171–183.

Council of Regional Accrediting Commissions. (n.d.). *Regional accreditation and student learning: Principles of good practices.* Washington, DC: Council for Higher Education Accreditation.

Curry, B. K. (1992). Instituting enduring innovations: Achieving continuity of change in higher education.(ERIC Digest No. ED35811, HEO26562). Washington, DC: ERIC Clearinghouse on Higher Education.

Dalton, J., Healy, M., & Moore, J. (1985). Planning a comprehensive values education program. In J. Dalton (Ed.), *Promoting values development in college students* (pp. 1–16). Washington, DC: National Association of Student Personnel Administrators.

Drucker, P. F. (2003). *The essential Drucker: The best of sixty years of Peter Drucker's essential writings on management.* New York: HarperCollins.

Drucker, P. F. (2006). *The practice of management.* New York: HarperCollins.

Ewell, P. T., & Jones, D. P. (1993). Actions matter: The case for indirect measures in assessing higher education's progress on the national education goals. *Journal of General Education, 42*(2), 123–148.

Geoghegan, W. H. (1994). What ever happened to instructional technology? In S. Bapna, A. Emdad, & J. Zaveri (Eds.), *Proceedings of 22nd annual conference of the International Business Schools Computing Association.* Baltimore, MD: International Business Schools Computing Association.

Gray, P. J. (2002). The roots of assessment: Tensions, solutions, and research directions. In T. W. Banta & Associates (Eds.), *Building a scholarship of assessment* (pp. 49–66). San Francisco: Jossey-Bass.

Gronlund, N. (2000). *How to write and use instructional objectives* (6th ed.). Upper Saddle River, NJ: Prentice Hall.

Grunwald, H., & Peterson, M. W. (2003). Factors that promote faculty involvement in and satisfaction with institutional and classroom student assessment. *Research in Higher Education, 44*(2), 173–204.

Hall, G. E., George, A. A., & Rutherford, W. L. (1977). *Measuring stages of concern about the innovation: A manual for use of the SoC questionnaire.* Austin: University of Texas Research and Development Center for Teacher Education.

Hall, G. E., Loucks, S. F., Rutherford, W. L., & Newlove, B. W. (1975). Levels of use of the innovation: A framework for analyzing innovation adoption. *The Journal of Teacher Education, 26*(1), 52–56.

Harding, L., Dickerson, D., & Kehoe, B. (1999). *Guide to outcomes assessment of student learning.* Fresno: California State University.

Hatch, M. J. (1993). The dynamics of the organization culture. *Academy of Management Review, 18,* 657–663.

Hatfield, S. (1999). Department level assessment: Promoting continuous improvement (IDEA Paper No. 35). Manhattan, KS: IDEA Center.

Huba, M. E., & Freed, J. E. (2000). *Learner-centered assessment on college campuses.* Boston: Allyn & Bacon.

Huber, M. (1991). Organizational learning: The contributing processes and the literature. *Organization Science, 2*(1), 99–115.

Julian, F. (1996). The capstone course as an outcomes test for majors. In T. Banta, J. Lund, K. Black, & F. Oblander (Eds.), *Assessment in practice* (pp. 79–81). San Francisco: Jossey-Bass.

King, P. M. (2003). Student learning in higher education. In S. R. Komives, D. B. Woodard, & Associates (Eds.), *Student services: A handbook for the profession* (4th ed., pp. 234–268). San Francisco: Jossey-Bass.

Kotter, J. P. (1995). Leading change: Why transformation efforts fail. *Harvard Business Review, 73,* 59–67.

Lincoln, Y. S., & Guba, E. G. (1985). *Naturalistic inquiry.* Beverly Hills, CA: Sage.

Linn, R., & Baker, E. (1996). Can performance-based student assessments be psychometrically sound? In J. Baron & D. Wolf (Eds.), *Performance-based student assessment: Challenges and possibilities.* Chicago: University of Chicago Press.

Lucas, A. F., & Associates. (2000). *Leading academic change.* San Francisco: Jossey-Bass.

McGourty, J. (n.d.). *What middle states evaluators will look for.* New York: Wiley.

Merriam, S. (1988). *Case study research in education: A qualitative approach.* San Francisco: Jossey-Bass.

Miller, T. K. (Ed.). (2001). *CAS: The book of professional standards for higher education.* Washington, DC: Council for the Advancement of Standards in Higher Education.

Moore, G. A. (1991). *Crossing the chasm: Marketing and selling technology products to mainstream customers.* New York: Harper Business.

National Association of Student Personnel Administrators & American College Personnel Association. (2004). *Learning reconsidered: A campus-wide focus on the student experience.* Washington, DC: Author.

Nichols, J. (1995). *A practitioner's handbook for institutional effectiveness and student outcomes assessment implementation* (3rd ed.). New York: Agathon Press.

Palmer, P. J. (1993). Good talk about good teaching: Improving teaching through conversation and community. *Change, 25*(6), 8–13.

Palumbo, D. J. (1987). *The politics of program evaluation.* Beverly Hills, CA: Sage.

Pascarella, E. T. (2001). Using student self-reported gains to estimate college impact: A cautionary tale. *Journal of College Student Development, 42*(4), 488–492.

Peterson, M. W., & Einarson, M. K. (2000). Analytic framework of institutional support for student assessment. In J. C. Smart (Ed.), *Higher education: Handbook of theory and research* (pp. 219–267). New York: Agathon Press.

Program Assessment Consultation Team. (1999). *PACT outcomes assessment handbook and support.* Bakersfield: California State University.

Rogers, E. M. (1995). *Diffusion of innovations.* New York: The Free Press.

Rosen, D. M. (1984). Leadership systems in world cultures. In B. Kellerman (Ed.), *Leadership: Multidisciplinary perspectives.* Englewood Cliffs, NJ: Prentice Hall.

Sandeen, A. (1985). The legacy of values education in college student personnel work. In J. Dalton (Ed.), *Promoting values development in college students* (pp. 1–16). Washington, DC: National Association of Student Personnel Administrators.

Sedlacek, W. E. (2004). *Beyond the big test: Noncognitive assessment in higher education.* San Francisco: Jossey-Bass.

Torres, V., Baxter Magolda, M., King, P., Jones, S., Pope, R., & Renn, K. (2004, November). *Assessing student development: A complex construct requiring diverse methodological approaches.* Symposium presented at the annual meeting of the Association for the Study of Higher Education, Kansas City, MO.

U.S. Department of Education. (2006). *The commission on the future of higher education draft report of 8/9/2006.* Retrieved August 10, 2006, from http://www.ed.gov/about/bdscomm/list/hiedfuture/reports/0809-draft.pdf

Walvoord, B. A. (2004). *Assessment clear and simple: A practical guide for institutions, departments and general education.* San Francisco: Jossey-Bass.

Walvoord, B., & Anderson, V. J. (1998). *Effective grading: A tool for learning and assessment.* San Francisco: Jossey-Bass.

Wergin, J. (2003). *Departments that work.* Bolton, MA: Anker.

Wiggins, G. (1993). *Assessing student performance: Exploring the purpose and limits of testing.* San Francisco: Jossey-Bass.

Wolverton, M., & Gmelch. W. H. (2002). *College deans: Leading from within.* Westport, CT: American Council on Education/Oryx Press.

REFERENCES

Allen, M. J. (2004). *Assessing academic programs in higher education.* Bolton, MA: Anker.

American College Personnel Association. (1994). *The student learning imperative: Implications for student affairs.* Washington, DC: Author.

American College Personnel Association & National Association for Student Personnel Administrators. (2004). *Learning reconsidered: A campus-wide focus on the student experience.* Washington, DC: Author.

Astin, A. W. (1977). *What matters most in college: Four critical years.* San Francisco: Jossey-Bass.

Astin, A. W. (1991). *Assessment for excellence: The philosophy and practice of assessment and evaluation in higher education.* New York: Macmillan.

Astin, A. W. (1993). *What matters in college: Four critical years revisited.* San Francisco: Jossey-Bass.

Aviles, C. B. (2000). *Successful collaboration between student affairs and academic affairs with a graduate follow-up survey.* Buffalo, NY: State University of New York. (ERIC Document Reproduction Service No. ED446707)

Banta, T. W. (2004). Introduction: What are some hallmarks of effective practice in assessment? In T. W. Banta (Ed.), *Hallmarks of effective outcomes assessment* (pp. 1–8). San Francisco: Jossey-Bass.

Banta, T. W., & Associates. (2002). *Building a scholarship of assessment.* San Francisco: Jossey-Bass.

Banta, T. W., & Kuh, G. D. (1998). A missing link in assessment. *Change, 30*(2), 40–48.

Barr, M. J. (2000). *The handbook of student affairs administration.* San Francisco: Jossey-Bass.

Barr, R. B., & Tagg, J. (1995). From teaching to learning: A new paradigm for undergraduate education. *Change, 27,* 12–25.

Bender, B. E., Lowery, J. W., & Schuh, J. H. (2005). Expectations of multiple publics. In T. E. Miller, B. E. Bender, J. H. Schuh, & Associates (Eds.), *Promoting reasonable expectations: Aligning student and institutional views of the college experience* (pp. 204–225). San Francisco: Jossey-Bass.

Bennion, D. H., & Harris, M. (2005). Creating an assessment culture at Eastern Michigan University: A decade of progress. *Assessment Update, 17*(2), 7–9.

Bensimon, E. M. (2007). Presidential address: The underestimated significance of practitioner knowledge in the scholarship on student success. *The Review of Higher Education, 30*(4), 441–469.

Bloland, P. A., Stamatakos, L. C., & Rogers, R. R. (1996). Redirecting the role of student affairs to focus on student learning. *Journal of College Student Development, 37*(2), 217–226.

Bolman, L., & Deal, T. (1991). *Reframing organizations.* San Francisco: Jossey-Bass.

Bowen, H. R. (1977). *Investment in learning: The individual and social value of American higher education.* San Francisco: Jossey-Bass.

Bresciani, M. J. (2006). *Outcomes-based academic and co-curricular program review: A compilation of institutional good practices.* Sterling, VA: Stylus.

Bresciani, M. J. (2008a). *Are you using technology to assess learning or assessing learning to improve technology?* Keynote address at the meeting of the Southwest Institute for Learning with Technology, Flagstaff, AZ.

Bresciani, M. J. (2008b). Presenting general learning within a bottom-line business world, part 1. Retrieved from *Net Results: NASPA's E-Zine for Student Affairs Professionals.* http://www.naspa.org/membership/mem/pubs/nr/default.cfm?id =1642

Bresciani, M. J. (2008c). Presenting general learning within a bottom-line business world, part II. *Net Results: NASPA's E-Zine for Student Affairs Professionals.* Retrieved from http://www.naspa.org/membership/mem/nr/article.cfm?id=1650

Bresciani, M. J. (in press-a). Challenges in the implementation of outcomes-based assessment program review in a California Community College District. *Community College Journal of Research and Practice.*

Bresciani, M. J. (in press-b). An introduction to outcomes-based assessment: A comparison of approaches. In G. McClellan & J. Stringer (Eds.), *Handbook for student affairs administration* (3rd ed.). San Francisco: Jossey-Bass.

Bresciani, M. J. (in press-c). Understanding barriers to student affairs/services professionals' engagement in outcomes-based assessment of student learning and development. *College Student Journal.*

Bresciani, M. J., & Jacovec, L. M. (2009). *Meta-analysis rubric.* Retrieved August 22, 2008, from http://www.ncsu.edu/assessment/evaluation/meta_analysis_rubric .pdf

Bresciani, M. J., Moore Gardner, M., & Hickmott, J. (2009). *Case studies in implementing assessment in student affairs.* New Directions for Student Services, 126. Boston, MA: Jossey-Bass.

Bresciani, M. J., Oakleaf, M., Duncan, K., Nebecker, C., Barlow, J., Kolkhorst, F., & Hickmott, J. (2009, February). Examining inter-rater reliability for a research methodology rubric. *Practical Assessment, Research and Evaluation, 14*(13A), 1–7.

Bresciani, M. J., & Sabourin, C. M. (2002, February). Criteria checklist for an assessment program. *National Association for Student Personnel Administrators, Inc. NetResults E-Zine.* Retrieved from http://www.naspa.org/netresults/article.cfm?ID =392&category=Feature

Bresciani, M. J., Zelna, C. L., & Anderson, J. A. (2004). *Assessing student learning and development: A handbook for practitioners.* Washington, DC: National Association of Student Personnel Administrators.

Burke, J. C. (2005). The many faces of accountability. In J. C. Burke & Associates (Eds.), *Achieving accountability in higher education: Balancing public, academic, and market demands* (pp. 1–24). San Francisco: Jossey-Bass.

Cohen, A. M. (1998). *The shaping of American higher education: Emergence and growth of the contemporary system.* San Francisco: Jossey-Bass.

Colorado State University. (2004). Planning for improvement and change. Retrieved February 11, 2008, from http://improvement.colostate.edu/about.cfm

Colwell, B. W. (2006). Partners in a community of learners: Student and academic affairs at small colleges. *New Directions for Student Services, 116,* 53–66.

Craig, D. H. (2003). Not such strange bedfellows after all. *Journal of American College Health, 51*(6), 263–264.

Creswell, J. W. (1998). *Qualitative inquiry and research design: Choosing among five traditions.* Thousand Oaks, CA: Sage.

Creswell, J. W. (2004). *Educational research: Planning, conducting, and evaluating quantitative and qualitative research* (2nd ed.). Upper Saddle River, NJ: Prentice Hall.

Denzin, N., & Lincoln, Y. (Eds.). (2000). *Handbook of qualitative research.* Thousand Oaks, CA: Sage.

Donald, J. G., & Denison, D. B. (2001). Quality assessment of university students. *The Journal of Higher Education, 72*(4), 478–502.

Eckel, P., Green, M., & Hill, B. (2001). Riding the waves of change. In paper series of the ACE Project on Leadership and Institutional Transformation and the Kellogg Forum on Higher Education Transformation. Washington, DC: American Council on Education.

Erwin, T. D. (1991). *Assessing student learning and development: A guide to the principles, goals, and methods of determining college outcomes.* San Francisco: Jossey-Bass.

Ewell, P. T. (1991). Assessment and public accountability: Back to the future. *Change, 23*(6), 12–17.

Ewell, P. T. (1997, December). Organizing for learning: A new imperative. *American Association for Higher Education Bulletin, 50*(4), 3–6.

Ewell, P. T. (2002). An emerging scholarship: A brief history of assessment. In T. W. Banta (Ed.), *Building a scholarship of assessment* (pp. 3–25). San Francisco: Jossey-Bass.

Ewell, P. T. (2003, October). *Specific roles of assessment within this larger vision.* Paper presented at the Assessment Institute at Indiana University-Purdue University Indianapolis.

Ewell, P. T. (2005). Can assessment serve accountability? It depends on the question. In J. C. Burke & Associates (Eds.), *Achieving accountability in higher education: Balancing public, academic, and market demands* (pp. 104–124). San Francisco: Jossey-Bass.

Feldman, K. A., & Newcomb, T. M. (1969). *The impact of college on students.* San Francisco: Jossey-Bass.

Feldman, K. A., & Newcomb, T. M. (1994). *The impact of college on students.* Edison, NJ: Transaction Publisher.

Fowler, F. J. (1993). *Survey research methods* (2nd ed.). Newbury Park, CA: Sage.

Green, R. L., Jones C. R., & Pascarell, R. B. (2003). Encouraging buy-in to assessment in student affairs via professional development workshops. *Assessment Update, 15*(3), 3–5.

Guba, E., & Lincoln, Y. (1981). *Effective evaluation: Improving the usefulness of evaluation results through responsive and naturalistic approaches.* San Francisco: Jossey-Bass.

Haessig, C. J., & La Potin, A. S. (2004). Lessons learned in the assessment school of hard knocks: Guidelines and strategies to encourage faculty ownership and involvement in outcomes assessment. In T. W. Banta (Ed.), *Hallmarks of effective outcomes assessment* (pp. 42–46). San Francisco: Jossey-Bass.

Hirsch, D. J., & Burack, C. (2001). Finding points of contact for collaborative work. *New Directions in Higher Education* (116), 53–62.

Hurtado, S., Engberg, M. E., & Ponjuan, L. (2003, November). *The impact of the college experience on students' learning for a diverse democracy.* Paper presented at the annual meeting of the Association for the Study of Higher Education, Portland, OR.

Hutchings, P., & Marchese, T. W. (1990). Watching assessment: Questions, stories, and prospects. *Change, 22*(5), 12–38.

Jacobi, M., Astin, A. W., & Ayala, F. (1987). *College student outcomes assessment: A talent development perspective* (Report No. 7). Washington, DC: Association for the Study of Higher Education. (ERIC Document Reproduction Service No. ED296693)

Kezar, A. (2001). *Understanding and facilitating organizational change in the 21st century: Recent research and conceptualizations.* ASHE-ERIC Higher Education Report Series, *28*(4). San Francisco: Jossey-Bass.

Kezar, A. (2003). Achieving student success: Strategies for creating partnerships between academic and student affairs. *NASPA Journal, 41*(1), 1–22.

Kramer, G. L. (2007). Fostering student success: What really matters? In Kramer & Associates (Eds.), *Fostering student success in the campus community* (pp. 433–448). San Francisco: Jossey-Bass.

Kuh, G. D., & Banta, T. W. (2000, January–February). Faculty–student affairs collaboration on assessment: Lessons from the field. *About Campus,* 4–11.

Kuh, G. D., Gonyea, R., & Rodriguez, D. (2002). The scholarly assessment of student development. In T. W. Banta (Ed.), *Hallmarks of effective outcomes assessment* (pp. 100–128). San Francisco: Jossey-Bass.

Kuh, G. D., Kinzie, J., Buckley, J., Bridges, B., & Hayek, J. C. (2006). *What matters to student success: A review of the literature.* Final report for the National Postsecondary Education Cooperative and National Center for Education Statistics. Bloomington: Indiana University Center for Postsecondary Research.

Kuh, G. D., Kinzie, J., Schuh, J. H., Whitt, E. J., & Associates (2005). *Student success in college: Creating conditions that matter.* San Francisco: Jossey-Bass.

Kuh, G. D., Schuh, J. H., Whitt, E. J., & Associates. (1991). *Involving colleges: Successful approaches to fostering student learning and personal development outside the classroom.* San Francisco: Jossey-Bass.

Light, R., Singer, J., & Willett, J. (1990). *By design: Planning research in higher education.* Cambridge, MA: Harvard University Press.

López, C. L. (2002). Assessment of student learning: Challenges and strategies. *Journal of Academic Librarianship, 28,* 356–376.

Love, P. G., & Estanek, S. M. (2004). *Rethinking student affairs practice.* San Francisco: Jossey-Bass.

Lucas, C. J. (1994). *American higher education: A history.* New York: St. Martin's.

Maki, P. (2001). Program review assessment. Presentation to the Committee on Undergraduate Academic Review at North Carolina State University, Raleigh.

Maki, P. L. (2004). *Assessing for learning: Building a sustainable commitment across the institution.* Sterling, VA: Stylus.

Manning, K., Kinzie, J., & Schuh, J. (2006). *One size does not fit all: Traditional and innovative models of student affairs practice.* New York: Routledge.

Mentkowski, M., & Associates. (2000). *Learning that lasts: Integrating learning, development, and performance in college and beyond.* San Francisco: Jossey-Bass.

Moore Gardner, M. (2006). Envisioning new forms of leadership in Catholic higher education: Recommendations for success. *Catholic Education: A Journal of Inquiry and Practice, 10*(2), 218–228.

National Governors' Association. (1986). *Time for results: The governors' 1991 report on education.* Washington, DC: National Governors' Association, Center for Policy Research and Analysis.

National Research Council. (2001). *Knowing what students know.* Washington DC: National Academy Press.

Northern Arizona University. (2007). NAU enrollment management and student affairs AY 2007–2008 assessment project description. Retrieved February 12, 2008, from http://www.nau.edu/studentaffairs/assessment/assessproj.htm

Oregon State University. (2007). College of business. Retrieved July 5, 2008, from http://www.bus.oregonstate.edu/programs/austin_entrep.htm

Pace, C. R. (1979). *Measuring outcomes of college: Fifty years of findings and recommendations for the future.* San Francisco: Jossey-Bass.

Pace, D., Blumreich, K. M., & Merkle, H. B. (2006). Increasing collaboration between student and academic affairs: Application of the intergroup dialogue model. *NASPA Journal, 43*(2), 301–314.

Palomba, C. A., & Banta, T. W. (1999). *Assessment essentials: Planning, implementing, and improving assessment in higher education.* San Francisco: Jossey-Bass.

Papert, S. (1991). *Situating constructionism.* In S. Papert & I. Harel (Eds.), *Constructionism* (pp. 1–11). Cambridge, MA: MIT Press.

Paradise Valley Community College. (2007). Assessment project report. Retrieved February 12, 2008, from http://www.pvc.maricopa.edu/library/assessment/AssessmentProjectReportSpring2007.pdf

Pascarella, E. T. (2006, September/October). How college affects students: Ten directions for future research. *Journal of College Student Development, 47*(5), 508–520.

Pascarella, E. T., & Terenzini, P. T. (2005). *How college affects students. A third decade of research* (Vol. 2). San Francisco: Jossey-Bass.

Patton, M. Q. (2002). *Qualitative research and evaluation methods.* Thousand Oaks, CA: Sage.

Peterson, M. W., & Augustine, C. H. (2000). Organizational practices enhancing the influence of student assessment information in academic decisions. *Research in Higher Education, 41*(1), 21–52.

Pike, G. R. (2002). Measurement issues in outcomes assessment. In T. W. Banta (Ed.), *Hallmarks of effective outcomes assessment* (pp. 131–147). San Francisco: Jossey-Bass.

Rudolph, F. (1990). *The American college and university: A history.* Athens: University of Georgia Press.

Sanderson, R. A., & Ketcham, P. (2007). *Student affairs assessment case study: Oregon State University Division of Student Affairs.* Unpublished manuscript, Oregon State University, Corvallis.

Schuh, J. H. (1999). Guiding principles for evaluating student and academic partnerships. In J. H. Schuh & E. J. Whitt (Eds.), *Creating successful partnerships between academic and student affairs.* San Francisco: Jossey-Bass.

Schuh, J. H., & Associates. (2009). *Assessment methods for student affairs.* San Francisco: Jossey-Bass.

Schuh, J. H., Upcraft, M. L., & Associates. (2001). *Assessment practice in student affairs: An applications manual.* San Francisco: Jossey-Bass.

Senge, P. (1990). *The fifth discipline: The art and practice of the learning organization.* New York: Doubleday.

Stage, F. K., & Manning, K. (2003). *Research in the college context: Approaches and methods.* New York: Routledge.

Strauss, A., & Corbin, J. (1990). *Basics of qualitative research: Grounded theory procedures and techniques.* Newbury Park, CA: Sage.

Suskie, L. (2004). *Assessing student learning: A common sense guide.* Bolton, MA: Anker.

Taylor, F. (1911). *The principles of scientific management.* New York: Harper.

Texas A&M University. (2005). Assessment questions form. Retrieved August 2, 2008, from http://studentlifestudies.tamu.edu/documents/questions_form_files/Assessment%20Questions%20Form—dr.pdf

Thelin, J. R. (2004). *A history of American higher education.* Baltimore: Johns Hopkins University Press.

Tinto, V. (1975). Dropout from higher education: A theoretical synthesis of recent research. *Review of Educational Research, 45,* 89–125.

Tinto, V., Love, A. G., & Russo, R. (1993). *Building learning communities for new college students: A summary of research findings of the collaborative learning projects.* University Park, PA: National Center on Postsecondary Teaching, Learning, and Assessment.

Upcraft, M. L., & Schuh, J. H. (1996). *Assessment in student affairs: A guide for practitioners.* San Francisco: Jossey-Bass.

Yeater, E. A., Miltenberger, P., Laden, R. M., Ellis, S., & O'Donohue, W. (2001). Collaborations with academic affairs: The development of a sexual assault prevention and counseling program within an academic department. *NASPA Journal, 38*(4), 438–450.

Also available from Stylus

Outcomes-Based Academic and Co-Curricular Program Review
A Compilation of Institutional Good Practices
Marilee J. Bresciani
Foreword by Ralph A. Wolff

"This is an important tool in the movement to transform higher education. It recognizes and celebrates the diversity of American higher education by encouraging institutions to define for themselves the characteristics of effective assessment practices and develop genuine, meaningful processes that will contribute to the improvement of teaching, learning, and student development. It makes an important contribution to the scholarship of assessment by providing a research-based framework for merging student learning assessment processes with cyclical academic program review processes."—*Linda Suskie, Executive Associate Director, Middle States Commission on Higher Education*

Introduction to Rubrics
An Assessment Tool to Save Grading Time, Convey Effective Feedback and Promote Student Learning
Dannelle D. Stevens and Antonia J. Levi

"An excellent guide to those student affairs professionals who have articulated clear intended learning and development outcomes and sought ways to measure the degree to which students are mastering those outcomes."—*Journal of College Student Development*

"*Introduction to Rubrics* has two vital things in its favor. First, it is short, and second, it is packed with useful information. This book is an ideal resource for those who are just beginning to think about using rubrics. However, it is also very useful for those of us who already use rubrics but need to refine our applications or get new ideas about how to optimize their use."—*Currents in Teaching and Learning*

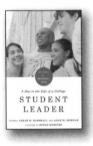

A Day in the Life of a College Student Leader
Case Studies for Undergraduate Leaders
Sarah M. Marshall and Anne M. Hornak
Foreword by Susan R. Komives

"The introductory chapter provides a brief and helpful guide about how to utilize the case studies: steps for analyzing key points, discussing stakeholders, and identifying possible courses of action. The authors also suggest different methods of use based on the reader's role: written assignments by faculty, or one-on-one discussions between the student leader and the advisor. This book works well as a teaching and student leader development tool."—*The Review of Higher Education*

The Assessing and Improving Student Organization (AISO) Program
Tricia Nolfi and Brent D. Ruben

The AISO program provides students with a structure for analyzing the workings of their student organization. It will generate insights to help them determine how effectively the organization is functioning, identify strengths and weaknesses, devise priorities and plans for future improvement, and in the process, promote students' reflective learning and leadership skills. The program consists of three elements:

Assessing and Improving Student Organizations: *A Guide for Students*
Assessing and Improving Student Organizations: *Student Workbook*
Assessing and Improving Student Organizations: *Resources for Facilitators CD-ROM*

22883 Quicksilver Drive
Sterling, VA 20166-2102

Subscribe to our e-mail alerts: www.Styluspub.com